THEIR DEADLY TRADE

Their Deadly Trade

Murders in Monmouthshire

Roger Williams

gomer

First Impression – 2004

ISBN 1 84323 389 4

Printed in Wales at
Gomer Press, Llandysul, Ceredigion SA44 4JL

With thanks to
JTW. JD.

'Silently, stealthily and presumably in the dead of night a crime has been committed which has sent horror throughout Monmouthshire.'

S.W.A The Llangibby Murders, 1878.

CONTENTS

The County of Monmouthshire has over the past few decades suffered from many changes. Not only has its boundary changed, but the old name, Monmouthshire, has been replaced by the original Welsh name for the area – Gwent. Since that time the county has been sub-divided into smaller administrative areas under the control of several different unitary authorities. For the sake of clarity within this book, the names Monmouthshire and Gwent are synonymous.

INTRODUCTION

Murder they say is as old as Cain. If this is so, then murder is the oldest recorded crime. Defined in the English dictionary as 'the taking of another person's life with malice and aforethought', murder is also the ultimate crime. And being the ultimate crime, British Law demanded, until 1965, the ultimate punishment – death by hanging.

Hanging as the judicial method of state execution was introduced into England by the Anglo-Saxons. It is believed that they in turn inherited this method of execution from their German forefathers. It was during the twelfth century, when Henry II introduced the Assize Courts and trial by jury, that hanging became the approved method of dealing with felons – *from about this time the statute books prescribed hanging as the punishment for all categories of murder, rape, treason, grand and petty larceny, burglary, and arson – along with 240 other crimes.*[1] At the beginning of the 19th Century more than 1,000 persons were being annually sentenced to death, although most of these were commuted by royal pardon.

By the fifteenth century the powers of trial, sentence and execution had passed mainly into the control of the larger towns, and in many areas actually into the hands of the landowners. These 'Lords of the Manor' imposed their authority ruthlessly, dispensing the death penalty, often using their authority to settle many personal grievances. It is a common belief that sheep stealers were tried, convicted and hanged at the Skirrid Mountain Inn near Abergavenny.

From the Middle Ages, death by hanging was almost always a public affair, great crowds would gather to see the barbaric spectacle being carried out. Unlike modern hangings, public executions were little more than death by slow strangulation. And it was not unusual for relatives of the condemned prisoner to bribe the hangman to speed up the end of their loved one by pulling on their legs to hasten death. In many cases it often took several hours for the unfortunate prisoner to expire. The State Executioner from 1874 to 1883 was William Marwood; he was the hangman who sent Joseph Garcia, the man responsible for the

The Skirrid Mountain Inn, supposedly scene of brutal judicial hangings. Marks on the beams in the bar are claimed to be from the ropes used to hang the felons.

Llangibby Massacre, to oblivion. During his term as official executioner, Marwood had invented the 'long drop'[2], a method of hanging, by which condemned prisoners were 'humanely' despatched. This was the first real scientific approach to executions. His calculations included both the weight and physical build of the ill-fated prisoner, and the length of rope needed to break the spine at the neck, thus causing instantaneous death. Prior to his calculations hanging could often be a grisly affair. Many prisoners were decapitated by the ferocity (length) of the drop and Marwood's system was introduced in an effort to avoid this 'outwardly and unnecessary mutilation of the victim's person'.

Prior to the 19th Century corruption was rife among the dozens of hangmen throughout the kingdom, most of whom were unskilled and recruited locally. From old reports we believe that in June 1744 Seth Parry was hanged in front of a large crowd outside the King's Head at Newport. He was executed for the murder of Caradoc Edwards of Henllys. From diligent research through the scant records which exist from that period, we also learn that the same Seth Parry was also considered responsible for the death of Carodoc's brother, Geraint

Edwards, even though the latter's death occurred some 11 years after Parry's execution. It appears that Parry had escaped death on the gallows. Rumours abounded that the hangman had been bribed to extend the rope, allowing the prisoner to drop to the ground below the scaffold where willing accomplices whisked Parry away, substituting a log for his body in the awaiting coffin.

Until their abolishment in 1868, public executions were a regular occurrence in Monmouth Prison. And from the middle of the eighteenth century, twenty-three criminals were publicly executed there while a further seven murderers faced the ultimate punishment on the gallows inside Usk Prison. The last Gwent man to hang met his end on the scaffold at Cardiff Prison in 1948. Since 13th August 1964[3] there have been no judicial executions in the United Kingdom. The end of the death penalty came with two executions, one at Manchester the other at Liverpool, which took place on the same day and at the same hour. And the last execution in Gwent took place at Usk Prison on March 23rd 1922, when William Sullivan[4] of Cwmbran, was hanged for the murder of Margaret Thomas who had lived in Llanover.

Until 1907 all local murder cases were investigated by County Police Forces. However, in that year a specialised 'Murder Squad' was established within the Metropolitan Police, and based at Scotland Yard. In a Home Office statement it was made clear that the Metropolitan Police viewed the investigations into serious crimes by their provincial cousins as inferior. The report also made it abundantly clear that there was no love lost between local forces and the Metropolitan Police. The report read, 'The County Police, excluding a few large provincial cities, have no detective forces. They deal well enough with the ordinary run of criminal cases, but when a case of special application arises, they almost invariably muddle it . . . A Scotland Yard detective gets very little help from the local men who regard his intrusion with great jealousy . . . It would be a great advantage if the County Police could be induced to call in their services at an early stage.'

It is almost inconceivable that only a generation or two ago, a murderer, within weeks of being apprehended, could be tried, convicted and put to death without the lengthy investigations required today. Nowadays, long before the defendant appears in court, many months of careful police investigations as well as meticulous legal preparations are carried out to ensure a conviction. The present array of specialist equipment to assist in modern-day murder detection would have astounded the police forces of only a generation or so ago. The seemingly limitless dimensions of DNA fingerprinting, supported by state-of-the-art forensic science, allied to the power of computers, were unimaginable. Yet surprisingly very few of the murderers, who practised their deadly acts of violence in Gwent, actually escaped being brought to justice. This book records many of the most notorious, bizarre, and unsolved murders to have occurred within the bounds of Gwent.

CHAPTER ONE

CRIMES OF FEARFUL CHARACTER

1878
THE LLANGIBBY MASSACRE:
THE WATKINS FAMILY

1892
THE DEATH OF A WOMAN OF THE TOWN:
MARY CONOLLY

1909
THE TANK COTTAGE MURDERS:
CHARLES AND MARY THOMAS

1921
THE DRUMMING-UP TIN MURDERS:
MARGARET THOMAS

July 17th, 1878

The Llangibby Massacre:
The Watkins Family

The arrival at Newport Town Dock of a ship carrying a cargo of iron ore in 1877 was in itself an event of no great importance. After all, Newport was one of the major ports of the Bristol Channel, and well-used to the importation of iron ore to feed the furnaces of the industrial valleys. However, what was to make this shipment unique was the fact that it set into motion a chain of events that was to culminate in the most horrific bloodbath ever recorded in the annals of crime in Gwent.

Among the ship's crew, was a twenty-year-old seaman named Yusaf Garcia, the youngest son of a prosperous, land-owning farmer from Seville in Spain. Having discharged the ore at the docks, the ship's company was paid-off, and the young Spanish sailor decided to stay in Newport to see something of the local high-life. This action was the first link in that tragic chain. For events were to lead inexorably from petty crime to their horrific climax in the most wanton and savage murders.

It wasn't long before Yusaf, or Joseph as he became known locally, had spent his money and was forced into crime to pay for the necessities of life. He is known to have frequented the numerous bars and drinking dens which abounded in the Pill area of the town, and it is a safe assumption that he was forced to steal in order to survive. On September 25th that same year, Garcia burgled the home of David Williams at St Brides, an isolated cottage situated on the marshes on the outskirts of Newport. He was interrupted in his crime by the sudden return of the householder's wife who had been visiting a nearby neighbour. On her arrival home, the poor woman was startled to find that the front-door padlock and its securing bolt were lying broken on the ground, and that the door lay open before her. Cautiously she entered the house and found that the living room had been ransacked. Moving into the parlour, she was horrified to find a man hurriedly bundling together a parcel of clothing. Realising the danger of the situation the courageous woman nevertheless demanded that the intruder leave her house immediately and that he should give the parcel of clothes to her. Garcia pushed past the terrified woman, making his way out into the garden, refusing however to hand over the clothing. Mrs Williams, undeterred, followed and again demanded the return of the bundled clothing, to which the young sailor replied, *'Me no gaol!'* As he hurried away from the house, and the pursuing, irate Mrs Williams, Garcia discarded some of the stolen items, dropping them at intervals one at a time as he tried to distance himself and make his escape. Perhaps the trail of clothing was a deliberate attempt to entice the woman to some secluded spot where he could silence her. This will never be known. For the sound of angry voices attracted the attention of two brothers, Thomas and Samuel Sully, who were fishing nearby and they too joined in the pursuit. After a chase that lasted for more than two miles, the fugitive was finally confronted, and in a bid to evade arrest, he armed himself with a large stick, and threatened his adversaries. Help, however, was at hand when another local resident whose curiosity had also been aroused by the raised voices came to their assistance. Between them they were able to overpower Garcia and he was taken to Newport where he was handed over to the County Police.

Throughout his trial, which took place on October 17th, 1877, the prisoner, with the aid of an interpreter, continually protested his innocence. The case against him, however, was damning. And following the evidence given by Mrs Williams, the Sully brothers and a police constable, who presented the stolen items before the court, the young Spanish sailor was sentenced to nine months, jail with hard labour. He was sent to Usk Prison to serve his sentence and thus the second link in the chain of preordained events was forged.

Having served his sentence, Garcia was released from prison on 16th July 1878, and placed into the custody of two warders who were ordered to escort the released prisoner to the railway station. They were to ensure that he was placed on a train that would take him back to Newport, where the ex-convict might be faced with the possibility of deportation. Garcia however, had different ideas and before the trio had left the precincts of the jail, he had managed to evade his escorts and made an escape, whereupon he quickly disappeared into the surrounding countryside. His escape, as a penniless foreigner in an unfamiliar rural area, was the final link in that tragic chain of events. And in less than twenty-four hours the whole country would be shocked at the *Tragedy of Fearful Character* that had taken place in the very heart of rural Gwent. There are few words that can adequately describe wilful and wanton murder, but on July 17th 1878, the name Llangibby, a small, quiet village on the road from Newport to Usk, became synonymous with the words 'inhuman butchery.'

The Watkins cottage, scene of the Llangibby massacre, Gwent's most brutal murders. The cottage was demolished shortly after the murders.

It was a bright, sunny Wednesday morning. The local residents of this rural community were already up, and about their normal business. But the bloody hand of death had already touched the village. Before the day was out the whole nation was to recoil in horror from the dreadful murders that were about to be uncovered. The day began with the arrival of a young boy called Frank James, at the cottage of William Watkins, a contractual farm labourer. Frank had worked with Watkins the previous day, and it had been arranged for both Watkins and the boy to work at the nearby Llan Dowlais Farm that morning. However, when the farm labourer didn't arrive, the young lad, believing that William had overslept, made his way to the cottage. Immediately on entering the garden he saw the bodies of Watkins and his wife lying across the garden path near to the gate. Realising that the couple were dead, the terrified youth ran to his parents' home and informed his mother of what he had seen. To get help they sought aid at the nearby Cefn Llech farm. The farmer joined them and together, fearful of what they would find, the group returned to the cottage. Meanwhile, John Morgan who lived close by had also discovered the bodies; a quick examination revealed that both his neighbours had been murdered. Watkins's throat had been cut with such savagery that his head had been almost severed from his body. Thrown across the murdered man's face was a bunch of Sweet Williams. The flowers had been picked from the garden and strewn across the face of the corpse as if an attempt had been made to hide the hideous injuries. A short distance away from where he lay, and close to the garden gate, was the blood-soaked body of Elizabeth, his wife. She also had been the victim of a vicious attack, suffering the same horrific injuries as those of her husband.

Mindful that the dead couple had children, Morgan ran to the cottage in the hope of finding the three infants safe, but was appalled to find that the living room was filled with thick, choking smoke. The fumes were so dense that Morgan was unable to reach the stairs and was forced outside. By this time Thomas Day, landlord of the Fox and Hounds, had arrived and between them they managed to raise a ladder to the roof. With the aid of a bar Morgan was able to remove some slates and knock a hole in the plaster of the bedroom ceiling, thus ventilating the house. After a few minutes the suffocating fumes had dispersed sufficiently to allow both the innkeeper and Morgan to force their way through the remaining smoke. Making their way upstairs they entered the children's bedroom and there the full extent of the tragedy was revealed: for here was a sight which chilled their blood, an even greater horror than that which lay outside in the sunlit garden.

The three Watkins children, Charlotte, Alice and Frederick, aged eight, five, and four respectively, were found with indescribable wounds. Unlike their parents, who had head wounds indicating that they had been stunned before having their throats cut, the children had been brutally slashed and hacked to death . . . all of them suffering stab wounds to the chest. Charlotte however also had multiple knife-wounds to her back, and was found lying face down between the bed and a blanket box situated at the bottom of the bed. It appeared that the eldest child had tried to gain access to the window in a desperate bid for help. She had, however been prevented from doing so by the murderous attack which had resulted in the several grievous stab wounds to her neck and shoulders. The child had then been dragged back and dumped lifeless into the confined space where she was found.

To add even more indignity to the affair the murderer had set fire to the bed on which the pathetic little figures lay, as if attempting to erase his terrible crime. Within the hour of the terrible discovery, several villagers reported having seen a suspicious looking foreigner in the vicinity of the Watkins's cottage the previous day. One of their nearest neighbours came forward to say that she had seen the stranger lying near the hedge of the Watkins's cottage. Another, Mrs Ann Gwatkins, told the police that a man answering the description of a 'swarthy foreigner' had entered her garden the previous day to ask for a drink of water and had asked for directions for Newport. This would have been several hours or so after Garcia had been released from jail. Immediately a search was made for Garcia as he was considered to be the prime suspect and a description of the escaped prisoner was circulated to all police stations in the county. More sightings from further afield were reported to the police. At eight o'clock that evening a carter named Humphries, who carried the Royal Mail from Abergavenny, reported that a foreign-looking man had desperately tried to hitch a lift from him at Llantarnam. But because the man was unknown to him, he had refused. However, he remembered that the fellow had the sallow appearance of a foreigner.

Around midnight another sighting was made on the outskirts of the town by Constable Tooze of the Borough Police. He, however, failed to recognise Garcia who was walking along the Marshes Road in the company of another man. Although his suspicions were aroused, the man he saw was dressed differently from the description that had been

POLICE NOTICE.

DESCRIPTION OF

JOSEPH GARCIA,

Height, 5ft 5in.; rather slight, apparent age, 21; dark swarthy Complexion; very black coarse Hair standing up, not parted, growing low down forehead; Black Eyebrows and Eyes; Whiskers, Beard and Moustache, black and slight; is a Spaniard.

When discharged from Gaol, at 8 a.m. on 16th July, was dressed in a blue blouse, reddish Guernsey under; Dark Trousers torn about knees; White Calico Shirt; light Blue Worsted round Cap; Old worn-out Blucher Boots, heels quite worn down; was carrying a pair of Canvas Shoes tied up in a reddish Cotton Handkerchief.

When apprehended on the night of the 17th July, was wearing a Grey cloth Jacket; hard black Bowler Hat; heavy nailed half Navvy's Boots, CARRYING A WHITE PILLOW CASE FULL OF CLOTHES, ALSO A BUNDLE formed of a Blue Blouse containing other Wearing Apparel, also a A TIN MADE LOAF OF BREAD suspended by a string.

Any person who observed "Joseph Garcia" dressed in either dress as above described between the hours of 11 p.m. on Tuesday, 16th, and 11 p.m. on Wednesday, 17th July, is requested to communicate with the Police without delay

EDMUND HERBERT,
Chief Constable of Monmouthshire

26th July 1878

A poster issued in connection with Joseph Garcia, the man responsible for the Llangibby massacre.

issued; besides, the fugitive had been expected to arrive in the town from another direction. Unsure of himself, the police officer did not approach the suspect on this occasion. Later that night, however, he saw Garcia drinking from a water fountain at the entrance to the Great Western Railway Station. This time, believing the man to be wanted in connection with the Llangibby murders, Tooze sought the aid of Police Sergeant Macgrath, of the County Police. Macgrath, he knew, had been present at the trial of Garcia the previous year. After seeing the young Spaniard he made a positive identification whereupon Garcia was immediately arrested.

In the early hours of Thursday morning, the prisoner was taken to the County Police headquarters situated in Bridge Street and placed into a cell that stood beneath the stage of the Victoria Music Hall – later renamed as the Lyceum Theatre. Once in police custody the protesting Garcia was searched and any doubt of his innocence was quickly dismissed when he was found to be carrying several items of female clothing. These were later identified as belonging to Mrs Watkins. Wrapped up in the bundle the police also found the disassembled movement of a mantle clock. It had been noted by the investigating officers at the cottage that the household clock had been dismantled. And although the weights and pendulum of the timepiece had been found in the house, the gear train was missing. His other possessions amounted to very little, only a few small copper coins and several silver dollars bearing the mark of the Spanish Government. In one of his trouser pockets was found a small clasp knife, but this was considered too small to have been the murder weapon.

Of the clothes that Garcia was wearing, the shirt was found to be bloodstained. He was also wearing two pairs of trousers. The ones he had worn at the time of his discharge were wet and these were beneath the top pair. It was thought that Garcia had made an attempt to wash away incriminating bloodstains. This, as far as the police were concerned, seemed conclusive evidence against him. An interpreter was called in and the prisoner was formally charged with the murders of William and Elizabeth Watkins and their three children. On hearing the charge against him the young man openly wept, repeating over and over again that he had not 'done such a thing.' Some hours later he was transported to Caerleon to appear before the magistrates. As news of the capture spread throughout the town, a large crowd of people gathered outside the police station.

With such headlines as *A Tragedy Unparalleled in Atrocity in the Annals of Crime of this County* the newspapers had already whipped up a public outcry against the suspected murderer. In the eyes of their readers, Garcia was already considered guilty of the brutal killings. Such a public reaction made the police fearful that their prisoner would be badly mauled by the crowds who waited noisily outside. This led the authorities to believe that Garcia would not receive an impartial trial, such was the 'Lynching mood of the county'.

This 'Lynching mood' was further inflamed by the findings of the Coroner's inquest, held at the White Hart Inn on the following day, July 19th. The jury, and those attending the hearing, were shocked as the truly horrifying details of the murders were revealed. William and

Elizabeth had been bludgeoned insensible before their throats were cut. In both cases the carotid arteries and jugular veins as well as the muscles of the neck had been severed with such ferocity that the head were left attached to the body only by the vertebrae. In the children's case however, they would have been fully conscious during the attacks upon them, and it appeared that 'each child had been stabbed and silenced in death in a similar mode to their parents.'

The intense silence that filled the makeshift courtroom was broken only by the audible sobbing and gasps of disbelief of those present. The doctor who had performed the autopsy described the terrible wounds that had been inflicted upon the three children. The fire that had been deliberately lit in the bedroom, he informed them, had badly charred their limbs, in some cases to the very bone. The atmosphere of the court was charged with emotion which ran high, and it was almost without precedent that when the jury returned their verdict they found that the death of William Watkins and his family was the result of 'wilful murder by Joseph Garcia'. The man suspected of the massacre had been

The White Hart in Llangibby where the inquest was held on the Watkins family.

in police custody for only a day, but in the eyes of the friends and neighbours of the ill-fated family, indeed by the whole county, Garcia had already been tried and found guilty. Yet despite the fears of a prejudiced trial, Garcia was arraigned to appear before the Winter Assizes at Monmouth. However, it was pointed out that the Winter Assizes were more commonly held at Gloucester. The prisoner was then ordered to appear before the Learned Judge at that Assize Court.

On Wednesday, October 30th, 1878, Joseph Garcia was placed in the dock at the Four County Assize Court held in the Shire Hall, Gloucester, before Lord Justice Barnwell. The transfer of the case had been something of a relief to the Monmouthshire County Police who were of the opinion that the 'public-minded of the county were too excited to ensure that the prisoner would receive a fair trial'. The prosecuting attorney, Mr Bosanquet, presented the formidable evidence before the jury. One of the first witnesses to be called was Mary Ann Watkins, the eldest daughter of the murdered man. Mary told the court that on the day of the murders she had been at Usk where she was in service. She was able to recognize the items of female clothing found in the bundle that Garcia had been carrying as her mother's. She also identified the boots that the accused wore at the time of his arrest as belonging to her father. This was confirmed by the shoemaker who had supplied the boots to Watkins a few weeks before the murders. At the time of his arrest Garcia also had in his possession a loaf of bread, this was known to have come from the Watkins household. The bread had in its crust a deep indentation, which was found to match exactly a dented baking tin in the kitchen of the cottage. Further damning evidence was given by a watchmaker who identified the clock workings found on the prisoner as having come from the mantle clock kept in the living room of the cottage.

There were no witnesses called to defend Garcia, and his counsellor made an unemotional statement to the jury. He called into question the lack of motive that the prisoner had in slaying the Watkins family. He was totally unknown to them: therefore he had no reason to murder them. His client, he continued, could offer no explanation as to his possession of the incriminating items known to have been taken from the Watkins's cottage.

In his summing up the Judge told the jury that the prisoner had been indicted for the murder of William Watkins only, and not for the wife and children of the dead man. Should Garcia be found guilty then he would stand convicted of all five murders. The jury remained in their seats and after conferring for less than three minutes the foreman stood up and faced the judge. A great hush descended on the crowd of onlookers in the public gallery and in a clear voice he said, 'We find the prisoner guilty.' When asked by the Clerk of the Court if he had anything to say before sentence was passed, Garcia through his interpreter replied, 'I don't know anything about it.' Then placing the black cap upon his head, Judge Bramwell pronounced the sentence prescribed by law, the death penalty, after which, it was noted by all those present that the customary words, 'May the Lord have mercy upon your soul,' were omitted by the judge.

The morning of November 18th 1878 was an exceptionally fine morning. Although bitterly cold, the damp, early morning mist had given way, and it looked as if it would be a bright clear day. Garcia awoke early, at about 6.30am, by which time crowds had already assembled outside the gates of Usk Prison. In the condemned cell, Garcia seemed totally unaware that he was to be hanged, even though for some hours his cell was a hive of activity, with the comings and goings of the prison officials. A few minutes before eight o'clock Garcia was taken from his cell. Led by a Catholic priest and flanked on either side by prison warders, he was ushered along the corridor into the central court of the gaol where the gallows had been erected. The scaffold, originally constructed for the executions of John Frost and his fellow Chartists, stood but a few steps from the pinioning room where Garcia was first taken. Swiftly, Garcia's arms were tied behind his back, and he was taken immediately onto the scaffold and placed onto the drop. On seeing the gibbet, his resolve failed and Garcia paled 'as if life had already fled.' Such was his distress that he had to be supported by the warders. Throughout the few final minutes of his life Garcia stood, eyes closed and head rolling from side to side, protesting his innocence. Silently Marwood, the executioner, stepped up behind him, strapped his legs and placed the white cap over his head, carefully adjusting the noose. The hangman took several seconds to ensure that the rope fitted snugly. Then stepping back he placed a spanner onto the release mechanism of the trapdoor, gave it two turns and the man responsible for the Llangibby Massacre was 'hurried to eternity.'

Death was instantaneous, the observers noting that the rope quivered for only a few seconds. For an hour the corpse was left hanging at the end of the rope before being removed. The prison doctor examined the body and formally pronounced that all life was extinct, a jury sat to confirm that death had occurred following the lawful execution of the prisoner and a death certificate was written. Finally Garcia's 'swollen and disfigured' body was buried in an unmarked grave within the walls of the prison.

In some people's minds, doubts about the young Spaniard's innocence continued for some time after his death – especially as he had maintained his innocence up until the moment of his death. But the evidence against him was overwhelming, and throughout his trial he had offered no explanation as to how he had obtained the clothing, bread, and workings of the family clock. It might seem strange to us in this day and age that Garcia's guilt should be so widely proclaimed, long before he was tried and convicted. Today such media coverage would not be allowed.

Although some doubted the guilt of Garcia, the greater majority were convinced that justice had been done. On the day of the hanging more than a hundred people gathered outside the gates of the prison, and at one o'clock William Marwood, the public executioner, came out to a tumultuous welcome from the waiting crowd. He was accompanied all the way to the railway station by the cheering throng. The crowd continued their cheers until the train finally pulled away from the station.

Controversy however, still surrounds the brutal murders more than 120 years later. For in May 1994 an article appeared in the *South Wales Argus* which advanced an alternative theory to account for the horrific fate of the Watkins family. The originator of the story, William Watkins of Newport, claims to be the grandson of an illegitimate child born out of an illicit love affair between Garcia and Mary Ann Watkins, the eldest daughter of the murdered family. According to Mr Watkins, Garcia had met and fallen in love with Mary Ann sometime in 1876.

The gravestone at Llangibby Church. Raised by public subscription, it marks the last resting place of the five murder victims of the Watkins family 1878.

The result of their love affair was the birth of a child, his grandfather. Garcia, he claims, desperate for money to support the young mother and child had broken into a house, was caught and sent to jail. Nine months later on his release, he returned to the Watkins's house hoping for a reconciliation with the family, Mary Ann and his child. He was rebuffed, and in anger murdered the whole family. At the time of the murders, Mary Ann was only fifteen and was employed as a domestic servant by two sisters who lived at Usk. At no time in the preceding months leading up to, and including the hearing was there any link mentioned between the pair. At the trial the only evidence offered in Garcia's defence was that he did not know the Watkins family and therefore had no reason to kill them.

Some of the most important evidence leading to the conviction of Garcia, came from Mary Ann herself, with no mention of the alleged love-child. Surely if such a child existed, then a plea of 'a crime of passion' would at least have been made. Unfortunately the colourful account presented by Mr Watkins does not conform to the true facts of the case. His flight of fancy, in the cold light of the evidence available, mistook Garcia for what he really was, an opportunist thief, who when cornered had brutally silenced his victims viciously and callously to ensure again that *'Me no gaol!'*

16th September, 1892

The Death of a Woman of the Town:

Mary Conolly

The Abergavenny races were in full swing, and large crowds of spectators flooded into the thriving market town to watch the week-long events. The day before the races drew to a close one of Abergavenny's residents, Mary Conolly, returned home after being released from Usk gaol having completed a twenty-eight day prison sentence for being drunk and disorderly, a condition for which she was well known. Throughout the day Mary had toured the many public houses in the town to celebrate her release. She was accompanied by a man who was not known by any of the local inhabitants, although Mary herself was familiar to almost everyone in the town. Around 7.30pm that evening, Mary and her escort called at the Somerset Arms public house, and the pair entered the snug where she ordered a measure of whiskey and glass of beer. The spirits she drank herself and handed the beer to her companion who sat with his back to the landlord. The innkeeper exchanged a few words with the young woman before returning to his other customers in the bar. This was the last time he was to see Mary alive, for the couple quietly left the public house unseen by either the landlord or those customers frequenting the bar. Less than an hour later Edward Wilkins, a railway worker, on his way to work stumbled across a woman lying outstretched in the gutter. His first reaction was that the woman had fallen and he called out to a woman passer-by for assistance. Both stooped over the prostrate figure and Wilkins struck a match to see her face. The sight that greeted their eyes however, sent both recoiling in horror – for the prostrate figure was Mary Conolly, and her throat had been cut from ear to ear. The woman who had stopped to assist Wilkins, slumped to the ground in a faint, and with some difficulty he raised her up until she had recovered her senses, then together they made their way to the police station. However, the woman was in such a distraught state that Wilkins put her in a cab and sent the lady home. Wilkins was left to make the journey on his own, but before he reached the police station the railwayman met a policeman on his beat and having reported to him his terrible discovery, both men returned to the scene of the crime. Under the spluttering light cast by the policeman's 'bull's-eye' lantern the true horror of Mary's plight became all too apparent. Her throat had been cut with such savagery that it was almost detached from her body. Her blood had formed a large, crimson stain around her shoulders and her clothing was drenched in the congealing pool. Her hands and face were also stained with her blood. Reinforcements were sent for and an immediate search of the area was organised. However, because of the lateness of the hour, this was abandoned, and it was decided that a more thorough examination of the district should be left until morning when better light would aid the police in their search for evidence.

The lifeless body of the young woman was examined at the scene by Dr Steele, the County Police Surgeon, whose preliminary examination revealed that the 'face and body were quite warm.' On hearing this news the police began searching all the public houses in the immediate vicinity in the faint hope of finding a bloodstained murderer. Then the pathetic remains of Mary were carried to the local workhouse and placed in the mortuary. The police surgeon, who performed a more detailed examination of the body, accompanied the corpse.

Saturday morning saw the resumption of the police search and it was soon discovered that a trail of blood led from the gutter where Mary had been found into a nearby garden enclosed by a low wall. Inside the garden and on the side furthest from the road stood a small shed, and between the shed and the wall lay Mary's hat. The still easily-detectable gory trail crossed the garden wall, over the cabbages, and led directly to the shed around which the ground was heavily trampled and showed two clear sets of footprints, one set was large with square toes and because of their size and the depth of the impression they were assumed to have been made by a pair of man's boots. The other imprints, being much narrower and with a smaller heel had presumably been made by women's shoes. From a closer examination of the scene it was apparent that Mary had been attacked in the shed and that in the last few moments of her life, despite the dreadful mortal wounds, she had struggled across the garden over the low wall and into the road in a desperate bid to seek help. But all to no avail, for the poor girl died in the gutter where she had been found.

News of the murder had reached Newport by telegram late on Friday evening, and by word of mouth to the outlying districts of Abergavenny. The police searches, which took place on Saturday morning in and around the area of Mary's slaying, were hampered by the arrival of hundreds of sightseers. These morbid onlookers arrived by train, pony and trap, bicycle and on foot. Many came from as far away as Newport and Cardiff and throughout the day the crowds continued to visit the scene. Many of them took away mementoes of the murder by collecting sprigs of hedging, which grew along the enclosed garden; others even collected stones from the road on which the unfortunate woman had died. Public houses in the near vicinity reported a brisk trade as the curious thrill-seekers sought refreshment before making their homeward journeys.

Later that evening the Coroner, Mr J. P. Walford, held his court in the Union House, and the witnesses were called to give their evidence. Dr Steele gave details of the injuries which had caused the death of Mary Conolly. A massive wound had severed the woman's windpipe, and all the tissue back to the vertebrae had been cut through as well as the left jugular vein. In answer to the Coroner's questions the doctor confirmed that the injuries could not have been self-inflicted and that a sharp instrument, probably a knife, had presumably caused them. The deceased woman's general condition indicated that she had been well-nourished and all her organs were indicative of her having enjoyed good health. She had been fully clothed, but wore no 'under-drawers'. There was no proof of sexual intercourse having taken place. After hearing the evidence the inquest was then adjourned until the following Monday.

Police enquiries had provided a description of the man who had been seen with Mary during her daytime visits to the public houses around the town on the day of her death. The increased police activity throughout the town searching for the murderer brought an early arrest, when a man resembling the description of Mary's male companion prior to her death was arrested by Police-Sergeant Davies. However, although 'he had kept the company of the woman Conolly, and his dress and appearance coincided with the description of the suspected murderer, he was able to establish his whereabouts for the remainder of the evening after he had parted from the victim'. The suspect was subsequently released. On Sunday, much to everyone's surprise, a man walked into the police station and asked to see the Superintendent, as he had vital information concerning the murder. When he was taken to see the officer he confessed to the murder of Mary Conolly. The man identified himself as Thomas Edwards, an ex-soldier and, since his release from the armed forces, a casual labourer. After his admission he was arrested, cautioned and then interviewed. He readily told Superintendent Freeman that he had cut the woman's throat with an open razor, and gave directions as to where the murder weapon had been hidden. But because of the way in which he had concealed the murder weapon, Edwards suggested that he be allowed to accompany the police to retrieve the razor. This was done and the prisoner directed the search party to a hedge, which bordered the Abergavenny to Hereford Road. He had been drinking for most of the day and was unable to account for his whereabouts since he had committed the crime. Edwards was committed to appear at the Monmouthshire Assizes and was remanded in Usk Prison to await his trial.

On December 1st, Thomas Edwards appeared in the dock at the Monmouthshire Assizes before Mr J.C. Day. The trial lasted only one day. Reports which appeared in the local newspaper described the prisoner as 'being aged about thirty, a labourer of respectable appearance'. He was charged that he 'On the 16th September, 1892, in the parish of Abergavenny, did feloniously, wilfully and of his malice aforethought, kill and murder Mary Conolly.' The court reporter noticed that Edwards had a 'vacant air' look about him as he gazed listlessly about the courtroom. In answer to the charge he replied, 'Not Guilty.' The prosecution opened the trial and briefly told the jury that the prisoner and the murdered woman had been seen drinking throughout the day, frequenting several public houses; firstly at the Cross Keys Inn then later by a man at the Foresters Arms. 'The woman Conolly', he told the jury, 'was an unfortunate creature, a woman of the town'.

Witnesses were called and the story of Mary's last hour on earth was unfolded. The prisoner and his victim had been seen walking down Union Lane, the pair had turned into the Merthyr Road and disappeared into the Somerset Inn public house. After leaving the inn they were seen by several witnesses who each testified to the route the couple had taken prior to the discovery of the body. Police evidence related that by following the trail of blood it was apparent that the murder victim had crawled from the garden shed through a wire fence and into the road where she was found. Next Edwards's statement was read out to the court and it described in graphic detail how he had cut the throat of Mary Conolly. It also explained how he had wanted to go to Newport to 'to kill one or two there.' The court also learned that Edwards's mother was an inmate at Abergavenny Lunatic Asylum. The prosecution asked the jury to decide as to the prisoner's mental condition at the time of the murder. When Edwards took the stand he answered the questions put to him by his defence counsel in a quiet voice. He had, he told the court, been a soldier serving in the Shropshire Regiment and had had an honourable discharge from the regiment, and was in receipt of a small pension from the army. It was established that he had no previous convictions and had led an exemplary life until that fateful Friday. When asked if he knew Mary Conolly he answered, 'Yes. We were in a bar with a small window. I gave her money. She asked me to go along with her and she took me to some garden or field there. There were ferns there with a wire fence. She lay down and I cut her throat with the razor. I was not intimate with her. I knew her before about two months ago and she then took more than £2 off me. She had made me unwell.' Edwards went on to explain that about seven years previously the Commanding Officer of the Shropshire Regiment, Colonel Findal, had been murdered in Birmingham by one of the loose women. 'Since then I have always been against those girls. If I'd had a good chance I should have killed one before'.

Prior to the trial Edwards had been visited at Usk Prison by Dr Glendenning, the medical superintendent of the Abergavenny Asylum. His evidence to the court was that on all the three occasions that he had met with the prisoner he had formed the opinion that Edwards was of sound mind. The defence spoke of a history of madness throughout the family, Edwards's mother was insane. His grandfather was known to everyone in the neighbourhood as *Silly Davis*, while his uncle was a complete imbecile. Drink, too, could have easily accounted for the prisoner's actions. Following the closing speeches the judge told the jury that they must take into consideration the statement of the prisoner – a statement that he had made quite freely to the police, and that drink was no excuse for crime. Most importantly, it was Edwards's sanity that had to be established and not the sanity of his relations. The jury retired but in a short time returned to the courtroom. The verdict was guilty and Edwards was sentenced to death. Edwards had showed no emotion throughout his trial. Even when hearing that he was to hang, he remained unemotional, showing little concern as to his ultimate fate. Quietly he was led from the dock and returned to Usk Prison to await his execution. An appeal for mercy was made to the Home Secretary to overthrow the verdict. Much was made by the prisoner's defence lawyers of the condemned prisoner's mental health. But despite all their efforts on Edwards's behalf, a reprieve was not forthcoming. This however did not seem to affect the remaining last few days of his life. Reports appearing in the press related that the prisoner was sleeping and eating well, apparently unconcerned as to his impending fate. 'It appears,' the paper said, 'that he is seemingly oblivious to his terrifying position.' The execution was set to take place at Usk on December 27th, 1892. On the day prior to the hanging the State Executioner, John Billington, arrived at the prison to make his preparations. Later that night a crowd began to gather outside the grim walls of the prison and much discussion as to the rights and wrongs of the sentence, and guilt of the prisoner incarcerated inside was heard. As the public houses in the area emptied so the crowd steadily grew in number. Finally, about midnight the crowd dispersed, though many were intent on returning at daybreak the next morning to pay silent witness to the hanging. The day dawned, cold with the watery sun barely able to break through the early morning mist, nevertheless more than two hundred people had assembled at the prison gate by 7.30am. At 6 o'clock, Edwards had been woken by the warders and told to dress and make ready for the final visit from the Chaplain. A few minutes later, from within the prison walls a muffled bell began to toll, its sonorous tones being clearly heard in the still morning air. Following the visit of the clergyman, Edwards was transferred to a cell adjacent to the scaffold where the executioner was already present awaiting the arrival of the condemned man. Within moments his arms were bound behind his back. He was led from the cell to the scaffold which had been painted black. There, Billington made the final adjustments to the rope, and a last minute inspection of the trap. The white cap was placed over Edwards's head and the noose secured about his neck. At the stroke of eight o'clock he was moved forward onto the trapdoor and his legs were quickly strapped. Then stepping back, Billington slipped the securing bolt and Edwards dropped from sight. The taught rope quivered for a few moments then hung still. At two minutes past the hour a warder appeared on the prison walls carrying a black flag which bore in white letters the legend 'JUSTICE'. This was hoisted onto the flagpole, upon which some of the throng who had remained silent throughout the morning cheered, then the assembled crowd began to disperse. The body was left hanging for another hour as prescribed by law, after which time it was taken down and removed to the prison infirmary.

Photograph of the main gatehouse at Usk prison. During the 19th century it was once the practice to fly a black flag bearing the words JUSTICE above the main entrance after the execution had taken place within the prison walls.

There life was pronounced extinct and that death had been instantaneous. A few minutes before 10 o'clock the Coroner and his jury arrived at the makeshift morgue where they viewed the corpse, in order 'to identify the body and to satisfy yourselves that the sentence of the law has been duly carried out'.

As was usual in those days, the speed with which justice was carried out was remarkable. The trial, an appeal and finally the execution had all been accomplished with alarming swiftness. Justice under the Victorians was certainly quick and final.

November 11th, 1909

The Tank Cottage Murders:

Charles and Mary Thomas

The greed for another's money has always been a major factor in murder. And on November 11th, 1909, in the quiet village of Bassaleg this motive was clearly evident in the vicious double slaying that became known as the Tank Cottage Murders. The small cottage had been named after the large water tower that was situated at the rear of the dwelling, and was rented by an old couple, Charles and Mary Thomas. Charles was aged 82 and his rather eccentric wife ten years younger. The couple had only recently moved into the small, picturesque village of Bassaleg, having lived for many years in the Gate Lodge that had then served as the main entrance to Tredegar House, home of Viscount Morgan. Indeed it was Mary Thomas's reluctance to open the gates to the mansion's many visitors that led to the pair having to vacate the lodge and move to Bassaleg. To the local residents it was not surprising that Charles, even at such an advanced age, had, up until three months before the murders, been employed by the Estate Manager as an assistant woodsman. But years working outside had taken its toll on the old man and he had finally given up the work owing to his severe rheumatism. On his retirement Charles became eligible to receive the newly-available state pension, which he accepted. His wife Mary, on the other hand, cantankerous as ever, would not accept the state payment, claiming that it was charity. Her misguided pride would not allow her to take advantage of the government scheme – relying, she told friends, on their savings to see them through their old age. And it was these savings that would eventually lead to the death of both Mary and her husband.

The villain of this tragic story, William Butler, was cast in a very different mould from that of Charles Thomas. Butler was a tiler and plasterer by trade, although for several years he had been reduced to casual labouring and taking odd jobs about the village, particularly at the Tredegar Arms, where most of his money was spent in prolonged bouts of drinking. At sixty-one years of age Butler was reasonably new to the area, having arrived in Bassaleg a few years earlier. He had for a time lodged with a very respectable family, the Wests, at Woodland View (what is now 22 Caerphilly Road), the house being situated only a few yards away from Tank Cottage. During his stay at Woodland View, Butler showed the seedy side of his nature: a side that was soon to become evident when he paid his unwanted attentions to the family's eldest daughter. The young woman complained of his behaviour to her parents and Butler was ordered out of the house.

For the next few weeks he took up lodgings at the house of a friend, Robert Doody, who lived in James Street, at Pye Corner. It was while living there that Butler's 'furious temper and towering passion' was first witnessed. He had returned to the home of his former hosts after one of his heavy drinking sessions, and threatened all within the house, especially the young woman who had complained about his behaviour, with 'ruin, that would bring tears to their eyes'. Because of this disturbance and his aggressive manner, Butler was arrested and ordered to appear at the Newport Magistrates Court, Pentonville, in November, the summons having been issued for causing a Breach of the Peace, because of his threatening and violent behaviour towards the Wests' daughter. Evidence on her behalf was to be given by her employer, Mr Rickets the local Stationmaster, amongst others. However, before anyone could attend the Magistrates' Court, Butler had been arrested for the double murder of Charles and Mary Thomas.

November 11th dawned with a heavy frost and throughout the morning it remained bitterly cold. Neighbours of the Thomases' were not unduly concerned that the couple's curtains remained drawn. As the pair did not enjoy good health they assumed that Charles and Mary were 'having a lie-in'. However, as the day wore on, a growing concern was felt amongst the neighbours about the non-appearance of the old couple. Things were brought to a head when the local baker, Mr Harris of the Pontymyster Stores, made his usual call at the cottage. After receiving no reply to his repeated knocking, he called on the local policeman, Constable Baile, who lived a few doors away. The house was forcibly entered and the terrible discovery of the bodies made. Immediately a message was despatched to the Chief Constable of Monmouthshire, Victor Bosanquet, who arrived at the scene accompanied by Superintendent Porter and Inspector Barry. The South Wales Argus reported that 'the news of the crime received was at first met with incredulity, when found to be true, it cast a gloom over the whole village'.

Immediate enquiries were made throughout the neighbourhood, and the last positive sighting of Charles Thomas was on the previous day, when he had stopped to talk to the village blacksmith at about 3pm. The blacksmith, it appeared, was the last person, other than the murderer, to see the old man alive. The news spread like wildfire throughout the district, and within hours hundreds of sightseers began to descend on Bassaleg. Crowds gathered outside the cottage, and the policemen on duty in front of the house were hard-pressed to keep order. From the garden many of the ghoulish visitors plucked flowers as 'mementoes of the terrible event'. The inquest was held in the Tredegar Arms where the Coroner gave details of the horrific injuries inflicted upon the victims, who had been bludgeoned to death with a blunt instrument. The murder weapon was never found: even the huge water tank at the rear of the house, from which the cottage took its name, was drained – but all to no avail.

Following the inquest the bodies of the married couple were released for burial, which took place on November 16th, the couple being interred at Bethesda Chapel, Rogerstone, where they had for many years been regular worshippers. On the day of the funeral hundreds of people lined the road along which the hearse was to travel, and as a mark of respect for the two victims, houses along the route had drawn their window blinds. Such was the throng of people attending the service that the chapel could not hold them all. A huge crowd also gathered outside to listen to the moving service that was relayed by word of mouth to the hushed crowd.

Residents of the village were routinely questioned by the police, and after they had sifted through the many statements that had been collected, the finger of suspicion began to point to William Butler. The suspect was taken into custody for questioning. Butler vehemently protested his innocence claiming that he knew nothing of the murders. He told police that on the night of the murders he had retired to bed at around 7pm. Witnesses however told of the money that Butler had been seen spending freely on the night of the murders in the local public house. He was buying drinks for several of his friends, having what appeared to be a large amount of money. When taken in for questioning Butler's clothes were found to be bloodstained, and he was unable to explain how the blood had got onto his clothing. Neither could he explain a cut to his thumb, a slight injury that could not have produced the quantity of blood that would account for the bloodstains. As for the money, Butler claimed that he had won it gambling, but this could not be substantiated. With such evidence against him, Butler was formally arrested and sent for trial.

Photograph c1909 showing the Tredegar Arms at Bassaleg where the inquest of Charles and Mary Thomas was held.

Butler was brought to trial on Thursday, 25th February, 1910. Throughout the trial Butler was in good spirits and spoke frequently to his counsel. Indeed at one point he openly laughed in court after the prosecuting attorney made a slip of the tongue while cross-examining one of the witnesses. However, as the day drew on, the evidence given by each successive witness pointed irrevocably towards Butler's guilt. Caroline James of Pageant Terrace, Bassaleg, told the court how on the morning prior to the murders the defendant had asked her for a loan of five shillings. She had told him that she didn't have that amount of money, although she offered him a loan of sixpence. Later that evening, Butler had called at her home and had asked her father to lend him the money. On the day of the murder however, several witnesses had seen Butler with a substantial sum of cash. When asked how he had obtained this money Butler claimed that he had won £100 on the Derby by placing a £1 bet with an acquaintance, Frank Smith. However in the witness box Smith denied any knowledge of the bet, and said that he knew nothing of Butler's claim.

The County Analyst, George R. Thompson, of Newport, presented forensic evidence. In his evidence to the court, Thompson told of the forty or so articles the police had given him for close examination. Notably amongst these items was a shirt on which 'signs of blood were detected' and a man's jacket where several spots of blood were evident. The examination of these two pieces of clothing had taken several days of analysis, and as a result of his tests, Mr Thompson determined 'that the blood spots were of recent date.' A candlestick and several items of bedding were also identified as being bloodstained. The analyst also suggested that a cut on the sleeve of Butler's coat had probably been caused by a broken pane of glass at the home of the Thomases' which the accused had apparently broken to gain access into the house. The trial closed and the jury retired to reach their verdict. They left the courtroom at forty minutes past nine o'clock and fifteen minutes later returned with their verdict, 'Guilty'. Butler began cursing both the jury and the judge, and was so enraged that he fought with the two warders who stood beside him in the dock. Such was Butler's fury that it took several minutes to subdue his struggles. Finally, Inspector Monrow of Scotland Yard, who had sat quietly throughout the trial, rose and read out a list of previous crimes which Butler had committed. These dated from 1865 to 1907. The court heard that Butler had already served a ten-year jail sentence for theft. He had also been served eighteen months for 'burglariously' entering a house in Brecon, and on that occasion had been convicted while using the alias of Thomas Palmer.

The final act in the courtroom drama was described by one reporter: 'There ensued a painful, exciting, and deplorable scene with the placing of the Black Cap on the judge's head.' In a solemn voice as befitted the occasion Mr Justice Grantham pronounced the death sentence. 'James William Butler you are sentenced to be taken hence to the prison in which you were last confined, and from there to a place of execution where you will be hanged by the neck until dead and thereafter your body buried within the precincts of the prison, and may The Lord have mercy upon your soul.' Butler, looking pale and shaken, loudly pronounced his innocence and still struggling violently was led from the court and returned to Usk prison. It was ten minutes past ten o'clock. From the moment that the jury had left the court to consider their verdict to their return and the passing of the death sentence only thirty minutes had elapsed.

On March 11th Butler's appeal against his sentence was heard at the Courts of Criminal Appeal before their Justices Lawrence, Phillimore and Hamilton. The accused was not present. On his behalf his Council for Defence, Mr Sharwood, put forward the argument that Butler had not received a fair and unbiased trial. Acting upon his client's instructions Sharwood told the justices that Butler's lawyer at the trial had failed to ask questions that might have absolved Butler of the crime. One of the witnesses at the trial, a Mrs Doody, had not been recalled or her evidence re-examined, leaving doubts about Butler's innocence. Police Constable Baile, prominent in the original murder investigation, had not been questioned as to the fact that Mrs West held a spiteful grudge against the appellant and therefore her testimony was suspect. And finally, that the presiding judge at the trail, Mr Justice Grantham, had misdirected the jury during his summing up, thereby ensuring a verdict of guilty being brought against the accused. All the arguments for the appeal however were dismissed, and the death sentence was upheld. Butler was to hang within the month.

At 6 o'clock on the morning of March 24th, 1910, Butler was roused from his prison bed. Having dressed quickly he was moved to a smaller cell at the opposite end of the prison, this being the furthest side away from the town. An hour later two clergymen, the Reverend Alfred Hoad and the Reverend Mr Robson, entered into the cell to attend to Butler's spiritual needs. About this time those who were to witness the execution began to arrive at the prison gate, and amongst these were the Chief Constable of the county, Victor Bosanquet, and Dr Hackett, the police surgeon. The two ministers were joined by J. W. Thorp, the prison Governor at 7.45am. Then as required by law, custody of the condemned man was passed from the Governor to the Under-Sheriff of the County. It was at this moment that the celebrated executioner Pierrepoint, as servant to the Sheriff, took over. After Butler's hands were swiftly tied behind his back, the prisoner was led from the cell to the awaiting scaffold, a mere dozen or so steps away. The Reverend Alfred Hoad at this point began to show signs of great distress and had to be supported by his colleague the Reverend Mr Robson. The witnesses had already assembled at the scaffold that had been erected in a small recess at the end of the first-floor corridor along which Butler was brought. Once on the scaffold John Ellis, Pierrepoint's assistant, quickly secured the prisoner's feet with a buckled strap. After the placing of a white cap over Butler's head, Pierrepoint put the noose around his neck, ensuring that the metal ring through which the rope passed fitted snugly against the left ear. Having done this, the executioner stepped back and on the stroke of 8 o'clock slipped the lever that sent Butler hurtling through the trap, snuffing out his life instantaneously. As was customary, the body was left hanging for an hour before being removed to the prison infirmary where life was pronounced extinct. The body was placed in a plain elm coffin that had been painted black, and Butler was buried anonymously close to the wall where the scaffold stood.

Outside the prison a crowd of about a hundred had gathered prior to the execution. The crowd was unusually small for such an occasion; even so many had bicycled from Llanhilleth to witness the event, having begun their journey at about the time that Butler had been aroused from his sleep. A few minutes before eight o'clock, those waiting outside fell silent as every ear strained for the sound of the trapdoors falling. They were not disappointed, as the doors weighed almost five hundred-weight; the sound of them crashing open was plainly heard outside the prison walls. Indeed so loud was the crash that many of the expectant crowd flinched and dozens of startled cries were heard. From St Mary's church, a muffled bell began to toll, adding its sonorous tones to the solemnity of the occasion. However, unlike previous executions at the prison, there was no bell rung from within the stone walls of the gaol. Nor was there the customary raising of a black flag with the word 'Justice' emblazoned across it to inform those outside that the execution had indeed taken place. Instead a formal notice was attached to the prison gate, which simply read:

DECLARATION OF THE SHERIFF.
We the undersigned, hereby declare
that judgement of death was executed upon
William Butler in His Majesty's Prison at
Usk in our presence.
ALFRED E. BOWER Under Sheriff.
VICTOR BOSANQUET Chief Constable.
J. W. THORP Governor.
ALFRED HOAD Wesleyan Chaplain.

Shortly after 10.30am, a second notice was brought out and attached to the gate. This stated that Dr Ernest Hackett had examined the body of William Butler following the execution and had pronounced him dead.

A Coroner's Court was convened in the Governor's office and following the inspection of the body by the Coroner and his jury, a verdict of lawful killing by hanging, was pronounced. During the hearing the foreman of the jury asked if Butler had finally confessed to the crime for which he was hanged. He was told that the condemned man had remained silent on that matter. But they were informed that Butler had gone to the gallows with a firm step, despite the fact that he was an old man, having, as the Governor said, shown an 'iron will throughout the whole affair'. Shortly afterwards the two State Executioners left the prison and, accompanied by two warders from Manchester who had been present at the hanging to 'acquaint themselves with the procedure', walked through the town to the railway station. Those who had continued to wait outside the gaol after the execution followed the group at a respectful distance and in total silence, only to disperse when the train had finally left the town.

26th October, 1921.

The Drumming-Up Tin Murder:

Margaret Thomas

When morning broke on Wednesday, 26th October, 1921, it was a predictable start to the day for David Thomas and his wife Margaret. The couple lived at Lapstone Cottage, a small stone-built house on the Llanover Estate, at Pencroesoped near Abergavenny. Having risen as usual just before 6am, David washed and readied himself for work, while his 48 year-old wife prepared their breakfast of fried potatoes and bacon. This finished, and having exchanged their goodbyes, David Thomas left for work. It was 6.45am. Little did he realize that this was the last time he was ever to see his wife alive again.

David worked at Ffawydden Quarry about a mile and a half from his home. There he was responsible for the removal of topsoil prior to the quarrying of the stone. It was an isolated spot and he made the journey alone, only passing at a distance one other of the estate employees, to whom he waved. Throughout the morning David cleared away the soil, occasionally resting to take a drink of cold tea. Following his mid-day meal he resumed his work, now and then passing the time of day with several other of the estate workmen who passed by. And it was late in the day when poor light forced him to finish off his day's tasks. David Thomas left the quarry and began the journey home, arriving at the cottage at about 5.30 p.m. He was not surprised when he found the cottage in darkness and the front door locked. He assumed that

Lapstone Cottage, scene of the Llanover Murder.

his wife had gone to the village to fetch some milk or groceries, as she had often done in the past. For a short while he sat on the low garden wall to catch his breath and await his wife's return. Sometime later he walked to the rear of the cottage and was dismayed to find that the pigs which were kept by the couple had not been released from their sty, nor had they been fed: indeed the same situation applied to the chickens in the coop. This was so different from the regular routine of the Thomas's household that a growing doubt as to his wife's whereabouts entered his mind. Having let out the animals, he returned to the house to collect the feed and noticed an open bedroom window. For the first time since arriving home David felt uneasy at his wife's absence. He knew that if Margaret had gone into the village she would have secured all the windows. Quickly he brought a set of ladders to the rear of the building and entered the darkened house through the open bedroom window. With him he took an oil lamp that was kept in the shed and in its dim yellowish glow he saw that the room had been ransacked. Making his way into the kitchen he was horrified to discover a body lying before the fireplace covered with a bed quilt and some small rugs – only a pair of legs were visible. Terrified he rushed back into the bedroom and returned to the outside and ran for help to his adjoining neighbour, Mrs Evans. Immediately the police and a doctor were sent for and David accompanied by two of his neighbours, returned to the silent, darkened cottage. This time the front door was forced open and the three entered the building. One of the group was nurse Blanche Saunders of New Tredegar, who was staying with friends in the village at the time. Extra oil lamps had been brought and in their pale light, the flickering flames laid bare the worst fears of those present. In a pool of congealed blood lay the covered body of Margaret Thomas. The nurse raised the edge of the quilt and felt the corpse for any obvious signs of life, but the body was deathly cold to the touch and completely lifeless. All about them was the chaos of a looted kitchen with cupboard drawers pulled out and their contents strewn about. It was clear that the room had been thoroughly and systematically ransacked. The group left the house and waited outside in silence for the arrival of the police.

   Police Constable Preece was first on the scene and he made a quick appraisal of the situation. Raising the quilt and mats he saw the brutal wounds that had caused the death of the woman – she had been savagely beaten about the head and face. Lying close to the body was an iron bar, some eighteen inches long, and this, he concluded, had been the murder weapon. Next to arrive at the cottage was Superintendent Barry, and at his request David Thomas re-entered the house to see if any of his or his wife's belongings were missing. A preliminary search revealed that several items had been taken, a silver watch belonging to his wife, a base-metal watch belonging to him, along with a blue suit, a waistcoat, a pair of trousers, a pair of boots, a tie, two razors and some shaving soap. Also missing was a small amount of cash, about nineteen shillings in total. By ten o'clock that night the Chief Constable of Monmouthshire, Victor Bosanquet had arrived as well as the County Police Surgeon, Dr Thomas Edward Lloyd of Abergavenny. Once at the scene the doctor examined the body, and confirmed that the victim was dead. In his preliminary report the doctor stated that his initial examination had revealed that rigor mortis was very pronounced, and that there were several severe injuries to the face and head of the dead woman. Close by lay the iron bolt that Police Constable Preece had seen

Newspaper cutting of Margaret Thomas, the victim of the Drumming-Tin Murder, and her husband, David.

and Dr Lloyd agreed that this was the probable murder weapon as it had blood, skin and hair adhering to one of its ends. The corpse was removed and taken away for a post mortem examination.

Rudimentary inquiries revealed that a tramp had been seen in the area during the two weeks preceding the murder. An immediate message was dispatched to all police stations throughout the county ordering searches to be made at all the doss-houses within a twenty-mile radius of the murder scene. But this was to prove to no avail. It was assumed that the murder had taken place shortly after the husband had left for work, as neither the pigs nor the chickens had been released from their respective enclosures. This was, David Thomas told police, the very first chore his wife would have done after breakfast. The inquest was arranged to take place on the following Friday evening at the Temperance Tavern, a local public house.

At daybreak on Thursday organized searches were arranged in the general area of Llanover village, although the police believed that the murderer had long since made his escape. Lord Treowen, owner of the Llanover Estate, was in one of the search parties scouring the area. A careful examination was made along the canal bank in case the murderer had discarded his bloodstained clothing, but this like the other searches was to prove fruitless; and the whole day ended on a disappointing note. Many members of the local community came forward as witnesses to be interviewed by the police. Their information brought to light a sequence of events that had taken place during the weeks prior to the murder. Several of the village's inhabitants had seen a tramp frequenting the towpath of the Brecon to Pontypool Canal, which ran close to Lapstone Cottage. Mrs Rosser of Llanover village had stated that Mrs Thomas, who worked for her part-time, had arrived late on the morning of October 13th last. She was concerned when she found footprints on the pavement outside her back door. Much to her alarm she saw a tall rough-looking man standing by the wood-shed door and although very frightened she had asked him, 'What are you doing there?' To which he replied, 'I'm looking for some stick to light a fire.' Mrs Thomas ordered him off her property, telling him, 'There are plenty of sticks on the canal bank!' At this the man left, and, after locking-up securely, Mrs Thomas had made her way to work. The encounter had so distressed Margaret that she told Mrs Rosser she would ask her husband to get a dog as an added precaution in case the man ever returned. Her fears were heightened two days later when she saw the 'same chap again' near the cottage. A local milkman, George Smith, had spoken to a tramp at 5.15am on the morning of the murder. He had last seen the vagrant walking along the canal bank towards Abergavenny and in the direction of Lapstone cottage. Smith's wife had also seen a tramp at about 8.30 that same morning.

Meanwhile back at Lapstone Cottage a further search of the house by the bereft husband was made at the request of Superintendent Barry. This fresh search revealed several clues as to the probable identity of the murderer. While looking through the downstairs rooms a 'drumming-up tin'[5] was found. And in the main bedroom Thomas discovered a coloured handkerchief. Margaret's purse containing a treasury note and loose change, and a second pair of boots were discovered to be missing. Two days later while tidying the second bedroom Thomas found further items that were believed to have belonged to the killer. Some old underclothes were found that were ragged and filthy dirty 'as if they had been worn for two years ', as well as an old pair of boots and some foot rags.

By Friday 28th the police had compiled a description of the man they were seeking in connection with the murder. They wanted to interview a middle-aged man of slight build. The suspect was wearing a blue jacket, cord trousers tied about his legs with string, a light-coloured cap, and was shod with heavy boots. Hopes were raised that the affair was to be brought to a speedy conclusion when the police arrested a sixty-two-year-old vagrant in connection with the murder. The suspect, John Coughlin, answered to the description of a man seen in the general area prior to the killing. But the former ironworker from Ebbw Vale was later released without charge. The news of Coughlin's release cast a further air of despondency over the residents of the Llanover Estate.

The Coroner's Court was held on the evening of Friday October 28th, and those present heard the formal evidence given by the police, and the County Police Surgeon, David Thomas also gave evidence. Dr Lloyd told the court of the results of the autopsy performed on the dead woman. Death he had concluded had occurred within an hour of her eating her last meal. And that death was the result of a series of violent blows to the woman's head and face. There were three blows to the face and eight to the scalp. The latter had fractured the skull and had caused heavy lacerations to the brain; this he believed was the cause of death. He also believed that the injuries had been caused by a blunt instrument and that the murder weapon was probably the fourteen-inch iron bolt found next to the victim on which human hair, blood and tissue were found. He concluded that the victim would have been rendered unconscious by the first blow and died within a very short time. The inquest was adjourned until November 10th. Newspapers reporting on the events at the Coroner's Court, told how 'the husband, being very distraught, had cried throughout his evidence'.

Three days after the discovery of Margaret's body on the Saturday morning, county police assisted by estate workers, again began a thorough search of the surrounding countryside. Shortly before midday a 'great Hue and Cry' was raised when a party of searchers flushed a man out from of the woods which surrounded the estate. An immediate chase ensued, but the man was able to evade his pursuers when he entered Mill Woods. A cordon was thrown around the woodland and police remained active in the area throughout the night in case the man was sighted again. But once more their efforts were to prove futile.

Margaret's funeral took place on Sunday, October 30th. The day was clear and already the cold snap of late autumn could be felt in the morning air. Yet despite the cold weather many thousands of sightseers lined the route from Lapstone Cottage to Saron Chapel at Goytre where Margaret was to be interred. The huge crowd, who stood in silence, had come to pay their last respects as the flower-laden hearse passed by. The narrow country roads were badly congested as hundreds of 'out-of-towners', some from as far away as Bristol and Cardiff, descended on the small village. They arrived by charabancs, cars, motorcycles and even on foot. Notable among the many mourners were Lord and Lady Treowen. The small chapel was filled to capacity with estate workers, as well as the friends and relatives of the dead woman. Dozens of floral tributes had been brought to the graveyard adding their brightly-coloured display to the sombre grey of the autumn day. Following the death of his wife David Thomas was unable to stay at his home and arrangements were made for him to stay with friends nearby. He had decided not to return to the house, and to sell off the fowls and animals kept at Lapstone Cottage. Weeks passed and, with no new evidence forthcoming, hope of catching the brutal killer of Margaret Thomas began to fade.

However, Sunday, November 13th was to prove the turning point in the affair. Fresh evidence was obtained by the police when Richard Grover walked into Pontypool police station and handed over a blue suit and a pair of boots to the desk sergeant. He told the police that his wife had bought the clothing from a tramp some days previously, and having read the description of the missing clothes in the local newspaper had brought the items to the police immediately. The items were quickly identified as those that had been stolen from Lapstone Cottage, and as the property of David Thomas. Grover could not give an accurate description of the tramp that had sold his wife the clothes, but agreed that he would easily recognize the man should he ever see him again. Immediately the police throughout the Eastern Valleys of Monmouthshire were alerted to be on the lookout for any vagrant resembling the general description issued. Under the supervision of Superintendent John Barry a concerted search was made and within four days a man was arrested on the mountainside above Cwmbran.

On the morning of Friday, November 18th, there was great activity at the Pontypool police station. Shortly after eleven o'clock the Chief Constable of Monmouthshire, accompanied by Supt Barry hurriedly left by car, returning an hour or so later with one of the female witnesses who had given evidence at the inquest of Margaret Thomas. An identification parade was arranged with several unemployed men from the town being brought into the police station to take part. An hour and a half later Nurse Saunders, who had also given evidence before the Coroner, arrived at the police station and another six men were brought into the station for the second identification parade of the day. By 2.30 p.m. the prisoner was brought before the town's magistrates and stood in the dock handcuffed to Police Sergeant Davies. The prisoner was identified as William Sullivan, 'a native of Cwmbran, but of vagrant habits'. Reports in the newspapers described Sullivan as 'below medium height, pale and unshaven, the accused appearing rather nervous, his lower jaw quivering throughout the hearing. He was dressed in ragged, dirty clothes. He wore boots but no collar'. The Clerk of the court read out the charge against the prisoner. 'William Sullivan you are charged that you did feloniously, wilfully and with malice aforethought kill and murder one Margaret Thomas at Goytre on October 26th.' When asked how he pleaded, Sullivan replied, 'Not guilty.' Superintendent Barry gave brief details of Sullivan's arrest, and asked that the prisoner be remanded until the following Monday. The magistrates agreed and the prisoner was led away. In total the whole hearing had taken only a few minutes.

Sullivan was again brought before the Magistrates at Pontypool on December 9th, and after an extensive hearing that lasted almost seven hours Sullivan was committed for trial at the next Monmouthshire Assizes. He was escorted from the court and taken to Usk Prison to await his trial.

Sullivan's trial opened at the Monmouthshire Assizes on February 8th, 1922, and although the public interest in the forthcoming trial was intense, he had attracted very little attention when brought from Usk prison by train, accompanied by two prison warders. He was driven to the Shire Hall in a closed cab, and the few people who witnessed Sullivan's arrival at the railway station described him as having 'walked with a firm tread, but had looked unkempt with a stubbly grey beard of some days' growth. He was dressed in the same old clothes in which he appeared at the Pontypool Police-court, and wore an old cap and no collar.'

The trial was to take place in the Shire Hall at Monmouth, before Mr Justice Darling. Acting for the Crown Prosecutor were Mr Arthur Powell, K.C., and Mr Lort Williams, M.P. Sullivan was represented by Mr S.C.R. Bosanquet, assisted by Mr Raglan Somerset. The jury, comprising of ten men and two women was sworn in. Immediately an objection was raised against one of the women jurors prior to the arrival of the judge. The Defence pointed out that the women in question lived close to where the murder had taken place, and prior knowledge of the crime which might result in her becoming biased against the prisoner. The arrival of the judge further complicated the issue, when he advised the two women that as the case was likely to extend over two days, they may wish to be released from jury service. He also added that as the trial would deal with matters which they might find distasteful, perhaps they should refrain from sitting on the jury. Duly advised, both women relinquished their places which were then filled by men, and the trial began.

The case for the prosecution was that on November 11th Sullivan had called at the home of a local miner, Mr Groves, who lived at 54 Albion Road, Pontypool. The vagrant was known to Mr Groves, who was a collier by trade, for he had once given Sullivan a cup of tea when he had called at the miner's house some months earlier. However on the day in question when Sullivan had knocked on the door it was opened by Groves's daughter. He asked the girl, 'Ask your mother if she wants to buy a jacket and a pair of boots.' The girl's mother then came to the door and said that she had no money, but Sullivan, whom she was later to identify, said he would leave the clothes and boots and collect them later that day. He had asked for two shillings for the coat and a half-a-crown for the boots.

Throughout the day the prosecution produced a succession of witnesses who were able to identify the prisoner as having been in the location of Lapstone Cottage a short time prior to the murder of Margaret Thomas. More damning was the testimony given by Sullivan's own brother as well as his brother-in-law. When placed on the witness stand they told the court how they met Sullivan on the afternoon of the day of the murder at the Forge Hammer Inn, Cwmbran; and how he, the accused, had bought them both three pints of beer each. The landlady of the public house was sworn-in, and she told the court that Sullivan had paid for the trio's beer with silver coins for the first round, and with a treasury note for the remainder of their drinks. When questioned about the topics of conversation, Kelloe, the brother-in-law, said that they had spent the afternoon talking about rugby football. Sullivan took his place in the witness box and was closely questioned about the money he had spent, the prosecution pressing him intensely as to how he had obtained it. Sullivan's answers were vague. He claimed that he had worked for a woman who had paid him the money, although he could not remember her name or where the woman lived. And so the questions continued. On several occasions the judge himself intervened during the cross-examination to clarify several points to both the jury and the prisoner.

But the most damning evidence against Sullivan was given by Mr Groves, the miner from Pontypool, who had bought the clothing and boots from the tramp. Having heard the case presented by the prosecution, Mr Justice Darling adjourned the trial until the following morning. Sullivan was duly returned to Usk Prison. The following day Sullivan was again brought to the Shire Hall under escort. On the journey from the station he had waved his manacled arms to several of his relatives who were walking to take their places in the court. By midday the trial had come to an end. It had been established that Sullivan, described as an unemployed 'Puddler'[6] had served in the army since 1901 being honourably discharged in 1919, since when he had not worked at any regular job. He had lived by journeying from one workhouse to another, working only at temporary employment when and where it suited him. Since his arrest Sullivan had maintained his innocence and although a vigorous defence was mounted on his behalf, there was a total lack of any corroborative evidence to establish his innocence. The jury retired, and two and a half hours later they returned to the court. Their verdict was 'Guilty of the wilful murder of Margaret Thomas'. The death sentence was passed and when asked if he had anything to say, Sullivan, looking drawn and pale, again protested his innocence, addressing the court in a clear ringing voice he said, 'I am not guilty, and have always said so!' He was then led away.

On Saturday March 10th, 1922, an appeal was lodged on Sullivan's behalf, however clemency was denied him by the Criminal Court of Appeal. The trial had been scrupulously fair, and it was his inability to provide a conclusive alibi, one that could be substantiated, that was given as the reason for the failure of his appeal. The execution date was set for March 23rd.

The arrival of John Ellis at Usk on the day prior to the execution was duly noted in the local newspapers. And on the following morning a small crowd gathered outside the prison gates. They stood in absolute silence waiting, they said, 'to hear the thud of the body falling through the trapdoor'. Shortly after eight o'clock a warder appeared at the prison gates and pinned a notice confirming that Sullivan had been executed. Some of the crowd dispersed, but a few remained until the Surgeon's Certificate was posted confirming that Sullivan had been certified dead. Shortly after 10 o'clock the notice was pinned to the wooden gates. It read:

Certificate of the Surgeon. 31 Vic. Cap. 24.

I E. L. M. Hackett, Surgeon of His Majesty's Prison at Usk, hereby certify that I this day examined the body of Wm. Sullivan, on whom judgement of death was executed in the said prison, and that by that examination I found that the said William Sullivan was dead.

Dated 23rd March 1922
Signed. E. L. M. Hackett

This was issued in accordance with the findings of the Coroner's Court held within the prison walls, a second notice accompanying the certificate simply stated that death 'was the result of lawful execution', and 'Death being due to the instantaneous dislocation and fracture of the neck vertebrae'.

Finally, having read the notices, the waiting crowds dispersed, satisfied that Sullivan had paid the ultimate price for the vicious murder of Margaret Thomas. As was customary Sullivan's body was buried in an unmarked grave within the prison precincts. He had the dubious distinction of being the last person to be hanged in Monmouthshire. The following year the scaffold was dismantled, and Cardiff Prison became the venue of all future Welsh executions.

CHAPTER TWO

THE INFAMY OF YOUTH

1920
THE ROSE COTTAGE SLAYING:
SARAH ANN WHITE

1921
THE ABERTILLERY CHILD KILLER:
FREDA BURNELL AND FLORENCE LITTLE

June 11th, 1920

The Rose Cottage Slaying:

Sarah Ann White

Sarah Ann White was a widow, described by her neighbours as an attractive, respectable woman, a person of modest, independent means, thanks to the foresight of her late husband. Sarah lived quietly at Rose Cottage, a picturesque, double-fronted stone building, situated in the tiny village of Llanfurin. Living with Sarah as a companion, was her fifteen year-old niece, Primrose Wistance. It was a breathless Primrose who arrived at the local policeman's house on the morning of June 11th, 1920, to report the death of her aunt. A preliminary inspection revealed that Mrs White had been brutally murdered. The Chief Constable was immediately informed of the details, and following the prevailing Home Office guidelines, he contacted Scotland Yard requesting the assistance of detectives from the Metropolitan Police Murder Squad.[7]

Photograph of Rose Cottage, scene of the brutal murder of Sarah Ann White, clubbed to death by her young niece, Primrose Wistance.

Meanwhile, the young girl had made a statement to the local police, describing the events leading up to the discovery of her aunt's body. She had, she told them, been woken by her aunt at about three o'clock that morning, and told to pack up her personal belongings and take them to her mother's house, a cottage about a mile and a half away. The girl had done as she was bidden, but because of the early hour, she had waited in the kitchen downstairs until it was light enough for her to make the journey safely. At about 5.30am she left, but returned a few hours later to Rose Cottage. Unable to find her aunt about the house or garden, Primrose made her way upstairs and on entering the bedroom, made the gruesome discovery of her aunt's blood-soaked body. News of the dreadful event soon brought newspaper reporters gathering in some number outside the cottage. And in answer to their continual clamour for information, the police finally informed the waiting newsmen that the crime had been 'a particularly hideous one – the victim having had her head battered almost to a pulp.' No further details were made available. The following day, reporters from the *South Wales Argus* interviewed the police, who informed them that they believed the murder to be the work of some stranger passing through the area, and that they were 'pursuing their inquiries with Unabated Vigour.' The reporters also spoke to the dead widow's niece whom they described as 'a bonny girl, rosy-cheeked, plumply-built, with large blue eyes, and an intelligent face.' The following day saw the arrival of the London detectives. Primrose was again questioned and a further statement was made confirming the discovery of the blood-drenched body of the widow. Following complaints from the press about the lack of information, further details were released to the waiting reporters. The murder weapon, it was revealed, was a heavy 'wooden stake beetle'.[8] Besides the large pool of blood found beneath the victim, bloodstains were also found splattered over the bedroom's ceiling, walls and furniture, all testifying to the ferocity of the fatal onslaught. It soon became apparent that the original police theory of the murder being the work of an outsider had been abandoned. None of the neighbours or villagers had reported seeing any stranger in the area. Details of Primrose's association with her aunt were also printed in the local newspapers. The girl, they reported, had been very happy living with her aunt, having moved into the cottage soon after leaving school the previous Easter. During her stay at Rose Cottage, Primrose had worked at the nearby Little Tyrhiw Farm that was owned by her uncle. To get about the village and to be able to ride to work, the aunt had bought the child a new bicycle only a week before the tragedy.

Neighbours stunned by the murder could offer no explanation for the crime, the widow, described as 'both attractive and respectable', had kept herself to herself, although she did occasionally receive male visitors. Several commented that 'Mrs White had a great fondness for jewellery', although this was not considered to be the motive for the slaying. Some confusion was caused by publication of an incorrect piece of reporting based on the original statement made by Primrose. The newspaper had claimed that the girl had in fact been away from her aunt's house for three days, and not a few hours as she had stated. In her second account of how she found the body the girl stated that, 'Auntie had told me to go home, but not to be gone too long, and to leave the door open. She had given me a gold ring as a small keepsake in case anything happened to her'.

The inquest was held on Monday, June 14th. Police evidence presented before the Coroner described the blood-splattered room, 'the victim still attired in her night clothes and the horrific injuries to the head and face, some being particularly vicious' – all showed signs of the victim's bitter struggle to evade her murderer. Immediately after the inquest Primrose Wistance was arrested by the London detectives. She collapsed, crying bitterly.

Appearing before Colonel J.A. Bradney, a local magistrate, at the Graig Cross Courthouse, Primrose was remanded until the following Saturday before being taken to the Pontymoile Mission House. On Saturday June 19th, she was again remanded for a further seven days, and formally charged with the murder of her aunt. Before being escorted from the courtroom she cried out, 'I did not do it. What makes you think I did?' Sobbing uncontrollably, and besieged by the press the young woman was returned to the custody of the Mission House.

Throughout the ensuing days the detectives continued to question their young prisoner. Damning evidence of her guilt had been collected and was presented before her. From her box of personal effects the police had retrieved five £1 notes along with a purse containing nine and a half pence. Finally Primrose Wistance broke down and confessed, 'I did murder my aunt.' She was formally cautioned, and her statement admitting the terrible crime was written down. It became known that her aunt had complained to her niece about coming home late one evening the week prior to her death. She had told Primrose that she must return home to her mother in the morning. The girl had had a heated argument with her aunt pleading not to be sent home, but the widow was adamant. The outcome was the vicious attack on the woman which resulted in the terrible murder.

Her trial was held on Saturday, November 6th, 1920, at the Monmouthshire Assizes, where she had been brought from Cardiff Prison. Primrose pleaded Not Guilty, but the damning evidence of her confession and statement, was overwhelming. The barrister for the prosecution pointed out to the jury that, under the Criminal Act of 1906, no child under the age of sixteen could be sentenced to death if found guilty of first-degree murder. As Primrose was under that age and if found guilty of the crime for which she had been indicted, then she could only be detained during His Majesty's pleasure – the place of detention being determined according the mental state of the prisoner in the dock. If found guilty but insane then she would become an inmate of an asylum for the criminally insane. If guilty and sane then she would be incarcerated in a secure environment suitable for a person of such years. This, he assured the twelve jurists, should relieve them of any pressure, knowing that they would not be sentencing such a young child to the gallows. The jury's verdict came quickly; Primrose Wistance was found guilty. Pronouncing sentence, the judge consigned the teenager to prison 'there to be detained during His Majesty's pleasure'. Sobbing loudly, Primrose was led from the court.

February 5th, 1921

The Child Killer of Abertillery:

Freda Burnell

The foreman of the jury stood up and faced the judge. Inside the court there was utter silence. In a clear, calm voice he read out the verdict of the jury. 'Not Guilty'. With those words the hushed courtroom erupted in loud applause and cheering. Caps were thrown in the air, as fifteen-year-old Harold Jones stepped down from the dock, free. The dark-haired youth, was quickly ushered from the court and taken into a side room, where an emotional reunion with his family took place.

The Shire Hall Monmouth where several notorious murderers were tried, including Harold Jones and Edmund Sullivan.

Outside the building a large crowd had assembled, waiting to congratulate the young man when he left the court house of the Monmouthshire Assizes. His appearance on the steps of the Shire Hall on that warm afternoon of June 21st, 1921, was greeted with more, and even louder cheers. He was hoisted onto the shoulders of several well-wishers and carried to a nearby hotel where a celebratory lunch was held. The toast was to *Freedom and Justice.* But, in the back of everyone's minds there remained one question, if Harold Jones was innocent of the murder of Freda Burnell, then who exactly was guilty?

Those who attended the one-day trial at the Shire Hall, Monmouth, had heard, through the dispassionate evidence of the police and expert witnesses, the sad story of Freda Burnell's last few hours of life. The drama that unfolded before those spectators who sat in the public gallery had begun on the morning of February 5th, 1921. It was a date that was to set an indelible mark on the small mining town of Abertillery, in the eastern valleys of Monmouthshire. Sudden and violent death amongst this close-knit mining community was nothing new; indeed most of the 38,000 souls who made up the population of the area were mainly miners and their families. To these, injury and sudden death was, all too often, a reality of life.

But what was to set this day apart from all others, was the disappearance of a young girl, Freda Burnell, while running an errand to a local shop for her father. It was an errand from which the eight-year old child was never to return. Concerned by the child's failure to return home, Freda's parents began looking for their daughter. As the morning wore on their concern grew, it was unlike the child to wander off. By midday the police were informed and they immediately organised a search, enlisting the aid of dozens of miners. The search quickly spread from the town out into the surrounding countryside where motor bikes were used to check the outlying areas. Throughout the day, and long into the weary hours of darkness, the men combed the hedgerows and isolated farm buildings that dotted the steep hillsides of this typical Welsh valley. Hundreds of sympathetic onlookers kept vigil long into the night. The progress of the search was noted by the movement of the lamps carried by the miners as they wove a thread of lights like a glittering, speckled necklace draped across the mountainsides. But, all their efforts were to no avail.

The early hours of Sunday morning saw the tired and hungry men returning to the town. While many came for some refreshment before resuming the search, all had come to hear the latest news of the progress in the hunt for the missing child.

It was in this pale light of day on that cold and frosty February morning that the pathetic remains of Freda were finally found. A miner on early shift was making his way to work along an unlit service lane at the back of Duke Street, when he saw what he believed to be a bundle of rags strewn on the ground. Closer examination however, revealed the terrible truth. The bundle was in fact the lifeless body of Freda.

Immediately the police were called to the scene and their preliminary findings revealed that the child had been bound and gagged. Her arms

The lane where the body of Freda Burnell was discovered. The X marks the place where the body lay.

were tied about the elbows and her feet secured tightly above the ankles with cord. She had been gagged with her wrap-around scarf which was knotted on her left cheek, and the marks of a violent blow to the side of her head were clearly visible. As was usual in those days, Scotland Yard detectives were called in to investigate the crime.

The murder investigation team arrived at Abertillery the following day and what was immediately apparent to the police officers was that the body had been found in an area searched on the day of the girl's disappearance. Its position on the open ground bordering the lane would have made it impossible to miss. A post-mortem examination revealed that Freda had probably died as a result of shock following a period of unconsciousness induced by a blow to the left side of her temple. It was also revealed that the dead child had been the victim of attempted rape. One of the first people interviewed by the detectives was Harold Jones, an assistant in the pet shop owned by Mr and Mrs Mortimer. It was to their shop in Somerset Street that Freda's father had sent his young daughter to purchase some spice and poultry grit. During the interview, the young shop assistant told the London detectives that Freda had called at the shop and had been served by him at about 9 o'clock on the Saturday morning. He added that he remembered her well, as she had been his first customer. He had sold the girl some spice and had asked if she required loose grit for their chickens, to which Freda had replied, 'I'll ask Ma.' The time of her leaving the shop, he guessed, would have been about ten minutes past nine. He had no idea of where she had gone after leaving the premises.

Over the next two days the detectives interviewed dozens of local residents as to Freda's whereabouts on the day she had vanished. Without success. Meanwhile forensic tests carried out on the body and clothes of the victim revealed several clues that were to aid the police in their investigations. Death was established as having occurred between 9.30am and 1.00pm on the 5th of February, the day she had disappeared. Adhering to the clothes were significant quantities of chaff, a substance normally associated with animal foodstuffs. Another vital piece of information that came to their notice was that the Mortimers rented a small storeroom that was situated in a nearby yard. On investigating the outbuilding they found that besides being used to

Mortimer's shop in Somerset Street, Abertillery, showing where Harold Jones worked.

house some prize fowls, it also contained a quantity of empty chaff sacks and poultry grit. They also learned that it was Jones's sole responsibility to feed and clean the birds, and what was more interesting, was that the young shop assistant was the only person with a key to the storeroom door.

A renewed and more thorough search of the small outbuilding was now undertaken. Almost immediately the close scrutiny revealed an axe handle secreted among the empty bags. But, what was to give proof positive that the attack had been carried out in the shed was a small white handkerchief that lay partly-hidden beneath some old boxes. It was soon established that the handkerchief had belonged to Freda's elder sister Ivy, who had a habit of chewing at the ends of the material, and her teeth marks were plain for all to see.

Forensic tests, although rather primitive at the time, did however reveal that a chalk residue was present on the handkerchief which Freda had borrowed from her sister Ivy. It was soon established that Freda had used the handkerchief to wipe the chalk from her toy blackboard,

The interior of the outhouse where Freda Burnell was murdered. The missed clue (handkerchief) lies on the floor near the door.

minutes before leaving for the shop on that fatal morning. Suspicion again focused on Jones. A witness had come forward to report that he had heard screams coming from the vicinity of the shed at around 9.30 a.m. on the day the girl had disappeared. Armed with this information and the fact that the handkerchief had been found in the outhouse, Jones was again questioned about the girl's death. However, he steadfastly refused to alter his original story, a story that was supported by the shop's owners themselves. They assured the police that Jones could not have left the shop at that time. Mr Mortimer himself, accompanied by his son Frank, had gone with the youth to the shed at 10.05 that morning. They were on their way to deliver a sack of animal foodstuffs, but had stopped to pick up a sack of potatoes from the lock-up. Mr Mortimer did admit that he thought it a bit unusual that Jones had left the hand truck outside the building, because it was usually trundled inside. Telling Frank to guard it, he went into the lock-up to collect the sack of potatoes which he carried out himself. After completing their deliveries, all three returned to the shop and remained there for the rest of the day.

Again the finger of suspicion was pointed towards Jones when the detectives discovered that on the night when most of the town's male population were out searching for Freda, Harold had gone to a friend's house to spend the evening there, having declined to take part in the search. After a few hours spent in the company of his friend, Jones left for home at about 11.00pm. However, it was nearly half an hour later before he finally reached home. The evidence although only circumstantial, was nevertheless an almost irrefutable indictment against Jones. The police concluded that, having murdered the girl on Saturday morning, he had waited until almost midnight before dumping the body in the lane, where it was found in the early hours of Sunday morning.

Jones was again brought to the police station and was subjected to intensive interrogation, but he continually refused to change his story. Finally after many hours of questioning he was formally charged with the murder, and subsequently appeared before the Monmouthshire Assizes on Monday, June 20th, 1921.

The trial aroused intense interest among the population of Abertillery and it was they who filled the courtroom on that day. The counsel for the prosecution opened the trial by presenting an expert witness who established the time and manner of death. This was followed by the police evidence describing how Harold Jones had both the opportunity and the means of murdering and secreting the body of Freda Burnell in a place that only he had access to.

Mr Mathews, counsel for the defence, called witnesses to testify to the good character of the accused. Finally, with all eyes fixed upon him, Jones himself was placed on the stand. Under cross-examination the young man proved impressive, answering all the questions in a clear, calm voice. Disregarding the suggestions put forward by the prosecuting attorney that he had murdered the little girl, Jones adhered firmly to the statement which he had made to the police, stating that he was innocent, and had not seen Freda after she had been served and left the shop. Then Mathews, turned to face the jury, and in a loud, firm voice asked, 'Is there any truth in the suggestion that you murdered Freda Burnell?' Jones replied with equal firmness and clarity, 'None at all, sir'. At which an audible sigh ran through the intent spectators.

In his summing up to the jury, the prosecuting counsel claimed that 'the evidence against Jones, although circumstantial, is enough to convict the boy for first-degree murder'. He also told them that the evidence they had heard, proved beyond all reasonable doubt, that Freda had died at or about 9.30am on that fateful Saturday morning, a time, he insisted, when Jones could have been absent for the few minutes required to perform this terrible deed.

Jones's counsel however, argued that many of the witnesses called by the prosecution had in fact added weight to his client's innocence. Hadn't the Mortimers, the boy's employers, confirmed that their shop assistant could not have possibly been away from the shop during the crucial time of the girl's death? 'If this is the case,' he concluded, 'then the prisoner must be totally innocent of the crime with which he is charged.' In his closing remarks to the jury, the judge was more than lenient towards the prisoner and, after little more than an hour of deliberation, the jury returned with a verdict of 'Not Guilty.' How soon were those twelve jurors to reflect upon their decision, and perhaps regret, for many years to come, their verdict.

The gravestone of Freda Burnell at Brynythell, Abertillery. Freda was the first victim of double murderer Harold Jones.

July 8th, 1921

Florence Little

Within a week or two life in Abertillery had all but returned to its natural rhythm. The murder of Freda Burnell a few months earlier and the recent trial, although still fresh in people's minds, had become the proverbial 'Nine day wonder'. The Jones's household at Number 10 Darren Road resumed its normal domestic routine, although Harold had not returned to work at the Mortimers' pet shop. Instead he divided his time between learning to play an organ, and trying to ride a bicycle. On July 8th, three weeks after the acquittal of their son, the Joneses, with their other children, decided to spend the evening with some friends and left Harold at home to look after his younger sister. Later that night the town of Abertillery was again the centre of a frenzied search for a missing child. While playing, eleven-year old Florence Little had gone missing from outside her home in Darren Road. Again hundreds of volunteers scoured the gas-lit streets and alleyways. Florence's mother had called at the Jones's house and asked Harold if he had seen her daughter. He replied that

10 Darren Road, Abertillery. The home of double murderer Harold Jones. The body of Florence Little was found in the attic of the house.

he hadn't, and volunteered to help in the hunt for the missing girl.
Search parties spread out into the surrounding fields, endlessly calling
out the child's name. All to no avail. It was decided, in the light of the
fact that the previous missing child had been found only yards away
from her home, to search the houses in Darren Road. No doubt the
implication of Harold Jones in the affair was paramount in the mind of
the police. Each house was inspected in turn; Police Constable Cox
entered Number 10 and within a minute called in his inspector.
Bloodstains had been found in the house, and in the attic, supported by
a rope tied around her waist, was the body of Florence Little. Her throat
had been cut. Jones was immediately arrested and taken to the local
police station, where he was charged with the murder of the girl. Within
minutes of his arrest hundreds of people had gathered outside the police
station, anxious to hear the details confirming Jones's arrest. Later he
was remanded to appear before the Monmouthshire Assizes on
November 1st, 1921.

Following the inquest, where it was disclosed that Florry 'hadn't
enough blood in her body to fill a few teaspoons', the funeral of
Florence took place on July 13th. A simple, moving service was held
in the family home. On the road outside and throughout the town,
thousands of sightseers crowded together in an effort to see the
proceedings. Several women fainted because of the overpowering heat
of the summer's day, and the milling crush.

It had been five months earlier when the public galleries of the
Monmouthshire Assizes had been filled to capacity. Even the benches
normally reserved for local journalists were full. The intense interest in
the trial that was about to take place had brought reporters from almost
every national newspaper. Regardless of the biting cold of that bleak
November morning those unable to get a seat in the crowded courtroom
again formed a large crowd in the streets adjacent to the impressive
stone building.

Yet, despite the crush of the spectators, both inside and out of the
court, the silence was overwhelming, as Harold Jones, for the second
time that year, stepped into the dock. This time however he was indicted
for the murder of eleven-year-old Florence Little. The child it was
reported had had her throat cut with such savagery that her head had

become almost severed from her body. And that, in an attempt to hide the body, it had been hauled into the attic of 10 Darren Road by a piece of rope taken from the backyard of the house. When asked if he pleaded guilty or not guilty, the accused answered in a clear calm voice, 'Guilty.' Loud gasps echoed around the courtroom.

Following a lengthy judicial argument a statement written by Jones was read to the court. In the hushed confines of the courtroom those present heard the chilling confession of the terrible crime:

'I Harold Jones do confess that I wilfully and deliberately murdered Florrie Little on July 8th, causing her to die without preparation to meet

Front Page of World's Pictorial News published after Jones's arrest for the murder of Florence Little.

Newspaper headlines following the arrest of Harold Jones for the murder of his second victim, Florence Little.

her God, the reason being a desire to kill. Florrie was about leaving the house when I got hold of her and seized her throat and cut it with a knife in the back kitchen, putting her head over the bosh.'[9] The statement continued to detail how Jones had carried the lifeless body upstairs and pulled the pathetic bundle into the attic, where it was later discovered by Police Constable Cox.

Jones, smartly dressed in a blue suit, linen shirt and knitted tie, was ordered to stand for sentencing. He showed no emotion nor remorse for his terrible crimes. In passing sentence the judge said, 'Words are not wanted and I think they are useless in this case. My duty is simply to pass upon you the sentence which the Act of Parliament has decreed should be passed upon anyone under the age of 16. That is you should be detained during His Majesty's pleasure.'

It was clear that Jones had escaped the hangman's noose because of his age. Had he been on trial two months later[10] it was almost certain that he would have faced the executioner. Having passed sentence on the prisoner the judge allowed a further statement to be read aloud in the court:

'September 17th, 1921. I Harold Jones, wilfully and deliberately murdered Freda Burnell in Mortimer's Shed on 5th February, 1921. Signed Harold Jones.' Jones was led from the dock without even a backwards glance, thus ending one of the most celebrated murder cases in the annals of Gwent's criminal history.

THE AFTERMATH

Jones was held in prison until after the outbreak of the Second World War. Because of the desperate shortage of men for the armed services, an amnesty was offered to many prisoners serving life sentences if they served in the military forces. Jones was one of the group of convicts who accepted, and he along with the other prisoners were paroled, joining a special army commando group – this company of soldiers was in later years likened to the fictional film characters known as *The Dirty Dozen*.

The group in which Jones served, formed an elite company of specialists, highly trained in the techniques of infiltration and sabotage.

Under the terms of their amnesty these 'specialists' undertook many hazardous and covert operations from which many were not expected to return. Yet despite these odds, Jones survived all of the dangerous missions in which he took part. And, at the end of the war, he duly received his parole, a proviso of which was that he did not return to his native town of Abertillery. However, it is rumoured that sometime in the 1960s Jones did in fact return home, perhaps in the belief that his crimes committed some forty years earlier had been forgotten or forgiven. But this was not so, he was recognised while drinking in one of the town's public houses. There followed a scuffle as several of the pub's regulars forced Jones out into the street. The police were called and Jones, as much for his own safety as for the disregard of the terms of his parole, was escorted from the town, never to be heard of again.

CHAPTER THREE

UNSOLVED MURDERS

1925
A Most Baffling Case of Murder:
Renee Watkins

1939
The Murder of a Well-to-do:
William Alfred Lewis

1959
Death on the Mountain:
Thomas Phillips

August 12th, 1925

A Most Baffling Case of Murder:

Renee Watkins

The evening of Wednesday, August 12th, 1925 was a particularly miserable one for August. The day had become prematurely dark as heavy storm clouds unleashed their burden of rain onto the Sirhowy Valley. But it was not just the weather that was to set this fateful summer evening apart from any other, but rather the sudden and inexplicable disappearance of Iris Watkins.

Iris, known locally as Renee, had left the house she shared with her mother and grandmother to post some letters in a postbox situated a short distance away from where she lived at Hillview Terrace, on the Cefn Road, Blackwood. The letter box was at the end of a narrow lane that led from Cefn Road to the High Street Square. Although normally lit, the pathway that night was in darkness, the only illumination was a meagre glow that filtered into the lane from the solitary lamp that burned outside the Pavilion Cinema. Even so, the lane was frequently used by the local residents, as it provided a shortcut from the town centre to the hillside residential area of the town. It was about 8 o'clock when Iris left the house to make the short journey to the square – it was a journey from which the twenty-two-year-old girl was never to return. By 11 o'clock the grandmother, concerned that Iris had not yet returned from her errand, sought the aid of her next-door neighbour, asking him to walk down the lane to the square to see if he could find Iris. But there was no sign of the missing girl.

Early next morning the police were informed of the young woman's disappearance. An immediate, although low key, police investigation began. From their enquires at the local post office they were able to confirm that the letters had indeed been posted in the letter box, a fact which increased the distress of the family and added to the mystery surrounding the whereabouts of the young woman. By midday there was still no news of the missing woman and the concern of both the family and police mounted. The original tentative investigation, supervised by Police Sergeant Davies, was widened. Under his direction police officers were ordered to broaden their enquiries to cover both the local bus and railway stations, but with no result. Wherever Iris had gone, she had not travelled from Blackwood by public transport. That she had left at all was in doubt, as there had been no preparation to this end. Her clothes were all accounted for, even her purse containing a few pound notes had been left at home when Iris had taken that fateful trip to post her letters.

As evening drew on the police received information that Iris had previously been keeping company with a young man from Tredegar, although it appeared that their relationship had ended some two or three months earlier. It was discovered that he had not been seen in Blackwood since the couple parted. Nevertheless enquiries were made and the ex-boyfriend, who had now moved from his home, was traced to Cardiff. Desperate for information, the grandmother and Iris's mother immediately travelled to the Welsh capital in the hope, if not of finding the girl, of at least learning of her whereabouts. The local newspaper, the *South Wales Argus*, had taken up the story and reported not only the concerns of the Blackwood police but also the fears of the distraught parent. For the mother, the only reason why her daughter had not returned home the previous night was that she must have been abducted. She believed that someone had bundled her daughter into a car and driven off with her. In an effort to obtain the help of the general public, the police had messages flashed on the screens of the three cinemas that served the busy township. The messages, asking for anyone with any information about the missing woman to come forward, received little response.

By the following Monday, August 17th, Iris had been missing for five days. Wild speculation and rumours had swept through the local community. The mother feared that her daughter had been seized. Her apprehension was tempered by headlines suggesting that the young woman had eloped, but if this was so, then with whom? Some suggested that Iris had had a 'tall secret lover', while others, showing more maturity, were concerned that she might have been a victim of an accident, perhaps having lost her memory, and was at that very moment lying injured somewhere awaiting help. No one at the time considered what was to be the tragic conclusion, that Iris had been murdered.

As the fifth day of Iris's disappearance drew to a close, the police, in an effort to trace the missing girl, had extended their enquiries. They had contacted and questioned the young man who had already been visited by Grandmother Watkins and her daughter. He categorically denied having any knowledge of Iris or her present whereabouts. At this point the police took a more intensive interest in the case of the missing girl. To add confusion to the case a witness came forward and told that on the night of Iris's disappearance he had seen 'a tall man and a girl, the latter in a raincoat but no hat, . . . in heated conversation beneath some oak trees in a lane leading up the mountainside from the road between Ynysddu and Pontllanfraith'. Nearby was a motorcycle which the witness assumed belonged to the man.

Immediately the public interest in what was now becoming known as the *Baffling Case of Renee Watkins* was fired with hints of scandal appearing in the local newspapers. Were the unknown woman and the tall stranger indeed Iris and her unknown lover?

With a week now passed and still no news of the missing woman, organised searches were made of the areas where the unknown couple had been seen. Although the countryside consisted mainly of rough terrain pockmarked by several disused quarries, a thorough examination revealed nothing. The abduction theory was now discounted and, with the aid of dozens of volunteers, the police mounted a second and more widespread search. Local woodlands, rivers and the small streams that coursed down the mountain sides were all carefully combed. Police officers waded through the icy torrents often waist-deep in water, but all to no avail. It was as if Iris had vanished from the face of the earth. Descriptions of the girl's appearance had been circulated throughout the South Wales valleys in the hope that someone, somewhere, might be able to throw light onto the case. Her description was published in every local newspaper, shown on cinema screens and displayed on posters throughout the valleys. Iris was described as being '5' 2" in height with dark, almost black, hair in a bobbed style; blue eyes and of small appearance: a person who carries herself well and looks intelligent'. Several appeals were made in the *South Wales Argus* for the as yet unidentified motorcyclist to come forward. But even this brought no response and the whole town took on an air of despondency. In the hope of keeping alive public interest, interviews with Iris's friends as well as the ex-boyfriend appeared in the local press – in addition to several headlines which speculated that Iris had been unhappy in Blackwood. It was the opinion of several people that Iris had for some time been discontented with her job at Tompkins, a newsagent and fancy goods shop situated in the town's High Street. She had, they claimed, obtained a new position in a nearby town and, not wanting any fuss, had just moved without telling anybody. Such idle speculation was quickly proven groundless. There was the matter of the girl's clothes and purse. And surely such widespread coverage of the girl's disappearance would have brought some response from the young woman herself. After all her mother was quick to announce that her daughter would never put her through such an ordeal. The whole matter was dropped and again the news faded from the pages of the press. As the second week came to a close renewed efforts to find the girl were made and full-scale searches extended as far as Machen Mountain, throughout the Rhymney Valley as well as in the Mynydd Islwyn area. Undergrowth and dense bracken were scoured by teams of volunteers, again yielding nothing new.

A bizarre twist to the mystery came with the arrival of a letter on the doormat of the Watkins's household. It read,

> *To Mrs Watkins,*
> *Don't worry about your daughter. She is quite safe at present and she will be returned to you unharmed if you put this letter in the daily papers. We kiddnapped your daughter to hold for ransom, but we know you are poor people, so we are returning her to you. Open your door at 2 o'clock a.m. on the 22nd of this month and you will find her outside cloroformed. I demand you to put this in the papers for the benefit of rich peoples daughters. If you don't do this you will never see your daughter again.*

The note was signed, *The Silent Strangers,* and included the post script, *Get it to the papers as soon as possible.* The letter was handed to the police and a copy of it appeared in the *South Wales Argus* on August 21st under the headline *Astounding News: was Renee Watkins Kidnapped?* The letter, however, was treated by the police from the very outset with caution. An analysis of the document revealed that it had been written on paper that had been torn out of a copy book. That the writer had made some attempt to disguise his handwriting, although some speculation as to the writer's ability to write fluently was raised. The punctuation, legibility, penmanship and spelling with the exception of the two mis-spelt words, *kidnapped* and *chloroform*, were of a high standard indicating its author to be an educated person. Sadly it was to prove a hoax, its perpetrator possibly gaining some perverse pleasure from raising the distraught family's hopes, only to have them dashed so cruelly.

By the end of the second week the spirits of the Watkins family were again lifted when a report appeared in the local press regarding a possible sighting of Iris and her secret lover. An assistant in a Newport shop thought she had recognised a woman who had been looking into the window of the shop where she worked as Iris Watkins. The window shopper had been accompanied by a tall man. As the pair looked at the display on show, which at the time consisted mainly of posters and various documents extolling the virtues of emigration to Australia and Canada, the woman had held a handkerchief to her face as if trying to avoid identification. The accompanying tall stranger had, throughout the whole incident, stood slightly behind the mystery woman. They had gazed into the window for several minutes before disappearing up Charles Street following the appearance of a police constable. The weeks dragged on and the mystery lost some of its news appeal. Little or nothing at all appeared in the papers. The whole case seemed doomed to be forgotten, until the morning of September 22nd when the truth about the whole mysterious episode of Iris's disappearance was to shock the valley town to its very core.

For several days during the previous week Blackwood and the surrounding area had had more than its fair share of rain. Many of the small mountain streams had been turned into rushing torrents as water cascaded down the steep hillsides. Catherine Tedstone and her husband lived in Brook Cottage, Cwm Gelli, a small house situated a short distance from the Blackwood Foundry. Just below the ironworks the stream that gave the Tedstones' house its name, emerged from a culvert. That morning Catherine accompanied by her husband had intended to walk the two miles or so into town to do some shopping. As they crossed a small bridge over the brook, Mrs Tedstone noticed a bundle of clothing a short distance downstream. She called her husband to go to investigate what it was. Tentatively he made his way to the place indicated by his wife. On reaching the bundle he at once realised that it was a body of a woman, naked save for a few tattered remnants of clothing and a Burberry raincoat that was wrapped around the head of the corpse. He had found the missing girl. Immediately the police were summoned, and the pathetic remains were briefly inspected for any signs of violence. Finding none, the police carried the lifeless body to a nearby shed to await the arrival of the police surgeon. It was assumed that the body had been lodged under the culvert where the heavy rain of the past few days had dislodged it, and washed it down to where it was found. News of the discovery spread through the whole community. The air was 'alive with rumours'. And hundreds of sightseers visited the place where the grisly discovery had been made. Some speculated that Iris had committed suicide; the reason to justify this speculation was, they whispered, that she had been pregnant. Certainly many young unmarried women in such a condition, living within a small community, would be driven by shame to such an end. But did this apply to Iris? If she had drowned herself why walk two miles out of town, and choose an isolated spot that was difficult to reach? Why hadn't she thrown herself into the nearby river that ran through the town? It offered a much better opportunity than a stream that at best would have been only a few inches deep.

Revelations made during the inquest were to astound everyone. Mr W. R. Dauncy, the Coroner, opened the inquest by calling for the person who had identified the body to step forward. Much to the Coroner's pique the witness (Iris's grandmother) was not in the courtroom. Police officers were despatched to bring the absent woman to the proceedings, as the inquest could not proceed without the identity of the deceased being confirmed. Eventually the distraught woman was found and brought before the Coroner. When asked if she had formally identified the body as her granddaughter, the old woman, who was barely able to speak because of her distress, told the Coroner that she had not seen the body. An aggravated Mr Dauncy informed those present in the court that he had given specific instructions that the body was to be physically identified and asked Police Sergeant Davies why these instructions had not been carried out. The sergeant confirmed that he had indeed relayed these orders but could not explain why they had not been implemented. When questioned further, Mrs Watkins said she had been able to identify a shoe and a remnant of the dress that Iris had been wearing on the night she had disappeared. A bracelet that had been found on the body was shown to the witness and she confirmed that it had belonged to her granddaughter. Further questioning revealed that she knew that her granddaughter had kept the company of several young men during the last year or so but couldn't remember if one of them had owned a motorbike. Next to give evidence was Dr Evans, who had made a preliminary examination of the body shortly after it had been taken to a shed near to where the girl had been found. He described how the body was practically naked. Hardly any clothing remained below the waist, other than a few wisps of her dress, her stockings and one shoe. Above the waist nothing but a few remnants of the girl's blouse remained. The Burberry that Iris had worn on the night she disappeared was wrapped around her head, with only one of her arms in its sleeve. The body itself was in a very advanced state of decomposition, 'and great changes had taken place'. The doctor estimated that Iris had been dead for approximately twenty days, although this was at best a considered guess. The head had suffered particularly badly from putrefaction, with most of the flesh and hair being absent. This made physical identification impossible. There was a natural lardy wax on all parts of the body where skin and flesh still existed. This would not be found if water had covered those parts. Much of the softer tissue had perished, and apart from the right knee being almost dislocated, there was no evidence of violence to the remains of the young woman. The skull along with every other bone showed no signs of fractures, and there were no visible indications of any penetrative wounds. All the signs which existed, he told the court, were in favour of the girl's virginity. From his investigations of the lungs he could positively state that the body had not drowned. The lungs contained no water. The Coroner ordered that owing to the lack of positive evidence indicating the cause of death, the internal organs along with the stomach and its contents should be analysed, for there was, he concluded, a possibility of poisoning. The court was then adjourned until October 8th, pending the analysis report.

News of the evidence given before the Coroner swept through the town like wildfire. Far from clearing up the mystery, the evidence only deepened it. Claims of suicide along with the belief that Iris had been pregnant could both be dismissed. Her body could not have lain in the water for any great length of time because of the waxy content of the remaining flesh. Iris had been missing for forty-one days, but at best the doctor could only guess that the girl had been dead for about twenty days. Yet the advanced state of decomposition belied this fact. There was no evidence of any physical violence that might have been responsible for her death. The whole of South Wales waited eagerly for the findings of the analytical chemists who were to present their evidence at the reconvened inquest. October 8th saw a large crowd attending the Coroner's court. In a hushed silence they awaited the results of the tests. First on the stand was Mr George Hogan, an analyst for the County of Monmouthshire. He was supported by a colleague Mr G. Thompson. Hogan in a clear voice told the Coroner that after carrying out a series of exhaustive tests there was no evidence to suggest that Iris Watkins had been poisoned. When asked to define exhaustive, he stated that both he and his colleague had conducted tests to determine if any acid or alkaline substances, along with any phosphorus compounds, hydrocyanic acid, compound carbolic acids, essential oils and acids in general, had been present in either the vital organs or stomach contents.

The police reported that after much investigation the driver of the motorbike had not been traced, nor had he acted as a responsible citizen and come forward of his own volition despite several appeals for him to do so. Summing up the proceeding the Coroner directed the jury to retire and consider the evidence that they had heard. After several attempts they finally returned to the court and read out their findings 'that the deceased had died as the result of wilful murder by some person or persons unknown'. The verdict did not meet with the Coroner's favour and he expressed this to the jury, adding that as this was the majority verdict then it must stand and he entered the findings into the record. The mystery of Iris Watkins's disappearance and subsequent death was never resolved. Many theories have been advanced, but none really explain what did happen on that wintry August night more than seventy years ago. If Iris was the victim of a murderous attack, then the killer can now be presumed dead, having taken his terrible secret with him to the grave. If this is so, then the mystery will never be determined, for like Iris and her killer, the truth has finally been laid to rest.

May 24th, 1939

The Death of a Well-to-do:

William Alfred Lewis

Following the demolition of Plasmont House, Pontypool, the final chapter in the building's tragic history closed. For not only was it the place where six members of the Lewis family had died, it was also witness to a suicide and one of Gwent's most mystifying cases of murder. The destruction of the house brought to an end its sad history, and a note of finality to the deadly secrets of the violent and unsolved killing that had taken place within its walls.

The old rambling, seventeen-roomed house had belonged to a wealthy local businessman, William Alfred Lewis. And it was William's battered body that was discovered there on the morning of May 24th, 1939.

Plasmont House stood in the shadow of Pontypool's Catholic Church. Its high walled garden dominated the junction of Upper George Street and Conway Road. A substantial structure, the building reflected the prosperity of its owner. For William Lewis owned a great deal of property within the town, some 200 houses and shops in the Pontypool area alone. The revenue brought in by these properties provided a substantial income to the fifty-nine-year-old bachelor, an income which could have provided William with some degree of comfort, but he chose to live a more austere lifestyle.

1939 saw the dark clouds of war gathering menacingly over Europe, and throughout Britain preparations for the oncoming hostilities were in full swing. The government, to ensure that the public were aware of the deepening crisis, had made available a supply of gas masks for every man, woman and child in the kingdom. And it was in order to collect his gas mask that William Lewis was seen at the distribution centre set up in the nearby George Street School. In the fitting room William discovered that the masks being issued were both cumbersome and uncomfortable, a fact that the businessman made known to those around him when he commented, 'I hope I shall never have to use this gas mask'. Shortly after his fitting William Lewis left the school building and walked the short distance to his home. It was 8.15pm. Little did he suspect that the brief walk would end in a fatal meeting with his murderer.

It was early the next morning when William failed to appear, as was his custom, when the curiosity of his neighbour, Mrs Barnett, was aroused. Normally William arose early and opened the kitchen door to allow the milkman to leave the milk on the kitchen table. On that fateful day the milkman found the door was ajar, as he expected; however, the previous day's milk still stood where he had left it and there was no sign of the occupier. Curious as to the absence of the owner, he mentioned the fact to Mrs Barnett whose cottage was attached to the main building. She poked her head around the door and called out. Getting no reply she enlisted the aid of Tom Brimble, a builder who was working in the grounds of Plasmont. Together they entered the house and again there was no response to their calls. Mrs Barnett, assumed that her landlord must have gone to Cardiff on one of his regular visits. Brimble however continued deeper into the house, and it was he who discovered the body of William Lewis sprawled across his bed. He had been battered to death.

The police were called and their preliminary examination of the murder scene revealed that William had severe head wounds and a pillow had been placed over his face. The bedroom in which the body lay had been ransacked. After questioning both the distraught Mrs Barnett, and the equally shocked builder, the police enlisted the aid of Scotland Yard. This was the standard procedure, all murder investigations nationwide were undertaken by detectives from the Metropolitan Police Force. Within a few hours several police officers accompanied by a Home Office pathologist boarded a train bound for Newport.

Their arrival at Pontypool late that afternoon saw a burst of activity at Plasmont House. In charge of the investigation was Detective Chief Inspector Rees, a detective with a formidable reputation for solving crime.

It was immediately assumed that robbery was the motive for the killing, although a tin box containing around £100 in sovereigns and a one pound note was found under the bed only inches away from the body. There were two safes in the house, both open and although containing no cash, they held property deeds and other documents. There was little indication that they had been rifled. However the house keys and those to the safes were missing. Detective Chief Inspector Rees in an impromptu press conference told reporters that both the keys and the murder weapon had not yet been found. He speculated that they had been taken by the murderer when he had fled the scene.

The inquest took place at the Coed-y-Gric Institute, Griffithstown at mid-day on Thursday, 25th May. Following the formal evidence given by the pathologist Dr Webster, a verdict of 'Death due to shock from injuries received' was entered. These injuries consisted of two contused wounds, one to the left temple and the other behind the left ear. Two fingers on the left hand were also badly bruised. These wounds, according to the pathologist, were probably inflicted while the victim slept. When questioned as to the possible murder weapon, he replied, 'Indications are that they were inflicted by a shoe' – probably one worn by the assailant.

1939 newspaper headlines reporting the murder of Pontypool bachelor William Lewis.

William Lewis was a well-known figure in Pontypool; he was described as a nice, shy man, who had been contemplating marriage. The whole town was alive with intrigue, and much speculation as to William's wealth abounded. A conservative figure of £50,000 was attributed to his personal fortune. Family members, notably his younger sister, estimated that more than £300 was missing from her brother's home. The money, she insisted, was the rents that William had collected a few days prior to his death. Sightings of two young men hanging about the general area the night before the killing were investigated, but the police were at a loss for any clue. The recovery of the missing keys caused some embarrassment for Chief Inspector Rees, when they were found in an attaché case belonging to Lewis in one of the rooms in the house. Messages asking for information concerning the murder appeared on cinema screens in the town, but to no avail. The police worked on the theory that he either had met someone as he walked home, or that someone was waiting for him in the house. Whatever the scenario, he had died within hours after he was last seen at the schoolhouse. In the major and lengthy investigation that followed, the house and its grounds were searched and re-searched, and police at one stage were digging in the gardens in a desperate effort to solve the murder. But their exhaustive endeavours to find the killer or killers led nowhere.

Local newspapers were scathing in their reporting of the murder investigation. The headline, 'Again; the murderer has walked away,' appeared in the *South Wales Argus* and it summed up the public's feeling that the police were incompetent. William Lewis was buried on Whit Monday, 1939. And the secret of the unknown hand that had slain him went with him to his grave. The news that now dominated the papers were the Royal visit to Canada and the U.S.A. and the general mobilisation as the threat of a European war grew more certain by the day.

A month after the murder the investigation was stepped down. A brief rekindling of interest was shown on July 22nd, when the contents of Plasmont House were sold off. But because of the nation's preoccupation with the impending war with Germany, the unsolved murder of William Lewis faded from the public eye. It has remained an unsolved and forgotten crime for more than sixty-two years. It is possible that the murderer is still alive, and if so, there is little doubt that he will take his secret with him to his grave.

March 4th, 1959

Death on the Mountain:

Thomas Phillips

It was one of the worst nights in living memory for those who lived on the bleak mountainside of Cefn Golau overlooking the small industrial town of Tredegar, high up in the Western Valley. It was not the sort of night that anyone would want to be out in. For Tom Phillips however it was different, he was concerned for the welfare of his herd of mountain ponies that was grazing on the mountain. With the storm growing worse by the minute he decided to try to round up as many of the horses as possible and bring them nearer the farm. He threw an old raincoat over his clothing and pulled on his wellingtons before leaving the house that he shared with his widowed mother, and his sister and brother. It was growing dark outside, but that did not deter Tom. That was the last time any member of his family saw him alive. As the hours passed the family became anxious at the continued absence of the young farmer. With the coming of the dawn the police were called, and in the pale morning light began one of Gwent's most baffling mysteries. Over the next three days police and local farmers from the surrounding communities of Rhymney, Tredegar and Abertysswg, searched the barren slopes for the missing man. All to no avail. As an explanation for the disappearance of his sibling, David Phillips was of the opinion that horse thieves might be responsible for his brother's disappearance. He told police that for three months prior to the mystery of Tom's disappearance, several of their horses had been stolen, but strangely all had been returned within a few days. And it had been the worry of further livestock thefts that had prompted Tom to try to round up the ponies on that fateful night. David's first reaction to the sudden disappearance was that the thieves had returned and waylaid his brother, leaving him injured somewhere on the mountainside. This idea was later dismissed when reporters from the South Wales Argus were told that 'Tom was a big man, well over six feet and quite capable of taking care of himself.' Those who knew the missing man agreed, for Tom, then in his mid-twenties, was at the height of his physical prowess, his body hardened after years of living and working on the windswept slopes of Cefn Golau.

Photograph of newspaper headlines during the search for the body of Tom Phillips.

Despite the draining of deep, mountain ponds and the combing inch-by-inch of the rocky crags, the continuing search yielded nothing. There was no sign of the missing farmer. As each weary party returned down from the mountain without news, it prompted the Argus to report 'the search goes on in one of the most baffling mystery stories which the town of Tredegar has known.'

After eight days of fruitless searching the police extended their hunt to the St James's storage reservoir situated some four miles from the Phillipses' Half Way House Farm. The reservoir at that time of year contained about 14 million gallons of water, far too much to drain. And it was here, close to the water's edge that the police came across their first clue, and it was one that did not bode well for the missing man. A corduroy cap, believed to be Tom's was found on the muddy bank. Rumours were rife but the next day, March 13th, any connections between the horse thieves and Tom's death were laid to rest when three men appeared before the magistrates in New Tredegar accused of stealing the animals. David Phillips was a principal witness against the men, but any thoughts that they were responsible for the farmer's disappearance were totally dismissed.

By now any hope of finding the young man alive had gone, indeed the hope of even finding his body waned with each passing day. Fate however, was to show her hand when on April 19th, forty-five days after his disappearance, the body of Tom Phillips was found. A man walking across the open mountainside saw what he described as 'a large bulky object floating in the reservoir'. Later that day the body of Tom was hauled from the water. On close examination of the corpse it was discovered that the hands and feet were firmly bound. Like wildfire, the news spread through the small communities: the missing man had, it appeared, been murdered after all. To the shock of the local inhabitants the police declared that there were no suspicious circumstances surrounding the discovery and they believed that the dead man had taken his own life.

Police Inspector Dan Plummer stationed at Tredegar police station was of the opinion that the dead man had taken his own life, a view that was also shared by some of his fellow officers. Police Sergeant Tommy Howells was the first to put forward the theory that Phillips might have committed suicide – a view that he was to maintain for more than 30 years. He later recalled,

'I was in charge of Tredegar Sub-division at the time . . . when I got up there [the reservoir] shortly afterwards and saw Tom Phillips hands bound in front of him, but I knew the family and was not going to jump to conclusions about murder.' He continued. 'Tom Phillips was a powerful man; I don't think anybody could have tied him up without hitting him and if they had done that there would have been marks on the body which would have been discovered at the post-mortem. People were afraid of the family but I don't think for a moment Tom Phillips had been murdered.'

All however did not share this point of view, Detective Superintendent David Thomas who was closely involved with the enquiry was convinced that murder had been committed, and many of

The bound hands of Thomas Phillips who was found drowned on Tredegar Mountain. Because of the way they were tied, considerable doubt was cast on the Coroner's findings.

The bound feet of Thomas Phillips. A public outcry was made when the verdict of suicide was given as the cause of death.

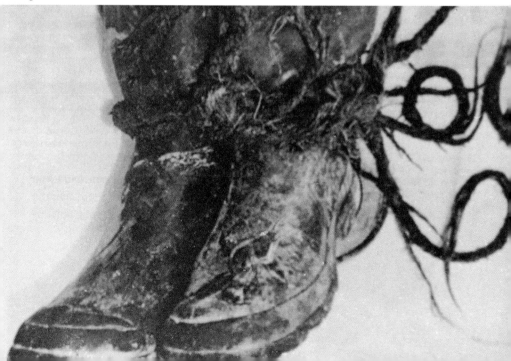

the local officers serving under him felt the same way. During the inquest details of the baffling case were made public. Tom's hands had been bound with a polka-dot handkerchief, which family members swore did not belong to the dead man. To add confusion to the whole affair a demonstration was given before the Coroner of how it was possible for a man to tie his own hands together. The demonstration carried out by a detective, who after 16 years as a scoutmaster must have been, according the Coroner, considered an authority on knots. This was as it may be, but the one question which remained on every one's lips was why would any man intent on suicide, venture out at night into one of the worst storms for years, then walk four miles to the reservoir, and tie his hands and feet before jumping into the water to kill himself?

Finally all the evidence and speculation had been presented, and those in attendance at the court waited for the Coroner's verdict. When it came it brought gasps of astonishment from everyone. The verdict was that Tom Phillips had taken his own life while the balance of his mind was disturbed. The family's protest at such a verdict fell on deaf ears. The answer to what happened on that bleak winter's night will remain a mystery.

This however, was not the first mystery to shroud the barren mountainside above Tredegar. In the early spring of 1940 a body was discovered near the banks of Cefn Golau Pond. The corpse was that of a messenger who worked at the Tŷ Bryn Institution, Tredegar. The dead man, of whom it was stated that he 'had performed his duties with great diligence' at the establishment where he had worked, was well liked by all that knew him. He had been missing for five months. When found at the water's edge, the body was fully clothed except for his boots. These were found tied tightly around his neck by the laces. At the inquest the Coroner's verdict was that the messenger had drowned, a verdict that surprised many. The isolated stretches of water on Tredegar Mountain it, seems, will eventually give up their dead but not, it appears, their secrets.

CHAPTER FOUR

MODERN MURDERS

1990
THE MYSTERY OF THE BODY IN THE BAG:
CLIVE TULLY

1994
THE RISCA TAXI MURDERS:
GERALD STEVENS AND CHRISTINE REES

1996
THE DEATH OF A SMALL TIME GANGSTER:
TYRONE FRANCE

March 21st, 1990

The Mystery of the Body in the Bag:

Clive Tully

March 21st, 1990, had started like any other day at the police station in Rogerstone village. Little did anyone realize that within a few short hours this small community would be propelled from its quiet backwater existence into the gruesome focal point of an international murder hunt that would stretch half way around the world.

At about midday a young police officer was despatched to investigate the report that two holdalls had apparently been dumped on the Rogerstone A467 by-pass a few hundred yards from the old power station. The bags had been abandoned in a lay-by and a passing motorist had reported them to the police 'as being suspicious.' On his initial inspection the police constable, Jeff Harris, discovered that the bags contained several parcels wrapped in polythene. To his horror he found that one of the packages contained what appeared to be human flesh. Harris later commented, 'The nearest thing to human skin is pig, but I knew it wasn't pig because of the texture of the skin and the hair on it . . . It turned my stomach.' The sudden realisation that he was apparently dealing with a shocking murder caused him to radio for help, and he was soon joined by a colleague. Having his suspicions confirmed by the second constable, PC Harris sent for Chief Inspector William Glynn, head of the Newport CID. Detective Chief Superintendent Mark Waters, head of the Gwent CID, joined them and immediately a major murder inquiry was set into motion. To co-ordinate the inquiries an incident room was set up in the Maindee Police Station at Newport. Meanwhile the bags with their pathetic remains were sent to the Cardiff Royal Infirmary where the grisly task of identifying the remains of what was once a human being was to take place. And so began one of the most intensive murder investigations ever undertaken in the whole of Wales.

The arrival of the body parts at the hospital where the autopsy was undertaken did little to raise police hopes of an early break-through in the murder investigation, for the body was incomplete. The torso and limbs were packed into the bags but the head and hands were missing. It now became apparent that not only did the police have to recover the remainder of the corpse in an effort to identify the victim, but also they had to look for the unknown dead person's murderer. At first the task of catching the killer looked almost impossible – without the head to aid in the identification, or the hands with the deceased's fingerprints that would enable the police to check records, and allow them to form some sort of victim-murderer association. As one spokesman commented, 'It looks pretty daunting.'

Under the skilled analysis of the forensics team, each of the individual packages were opened and from them were removed the mutilated remains. The first bag contained two arms from the elbow to the wrist, both without the hands, the right thigh, right calf and foot, and also the left thigh and foot. The contents of the second bag revealed the torso complete with its upper arms. Because both the head and hands were missing police assumed that his victim had known the killer and the dismemberment was a desperate attempt to conceal the identity of the headless torso. Early examinations revealed that the remains were those of a male aged between twenty-one and fifty years of age, although later examinations were able to narrow down the victim as being in his early twenties. His height and hair colouring were also confirmed. He would have stood about 5ft 7ins to 5ft 9ins tall, with gingery hair, and would have weighed approximately 11 stone. Amongst several other details to emerge from the autopsy was the fact that the victim had an extraordinary number of moles on his body: this was to prove a crucial clue in finally identifying the murdered man. A noticeable scar was found on the point of his right shoulder, although well-healed this would also become a further means of confirming the identity of the still as yet unnamed victim. His feet were heavily calloused, the torso and limbs deeply sun-tanned, although this was showing signs of fading. Evident throughout the pathologist's examination was the method used to dismember the body – a sharp bladed instrument had been used to slice through the flesh, and a saw was then used to cut the corpse into the smaller pieces. A breakthrough in the investigation came four days after the initial recovery of the two holdalls, when a farm worker found the missing head and hands. Andrew Newberry, a farm hand was helping with the spring lambing at Fair Orchard Farm, St Brides. Andrew had seen a red bag that had apparently been thrown into a drainage ditch along the St Brides coast road near St Mellons. When he examined the bag it contained what appeared to be a 'football shaped object wrapped in clear plastic' Feeling through the polythene he was startled to discover 'what appeared to be the shape of a nose and an ear.' Hastily the package was returned to the bag and after a few moments to get over the shock of the discovery Andrew phoned the police. The examination of the head revealed that it had been subjected to a frenzied attack having been dealt at least twelve savage blows probably with a blunt instrument such as a hammer. Fingerprints were lifted from the hands, although these were found to have no match anywhere in the extensive police records. The Art Editor of the *South Wales Argus*, Geoff Fowler, offered the police his services and using a photograph of the severed head, he was able to enhance the photo with the aid of the newspaper's computer. For the first time since the investigation had begun the police were able to look at the face of the still-unidentified man. From the plastic packaging used to cover the head, forensic experts were able to 'lift' fingerprints and these were to be the first vital clue in solving the case that had become known as 'The Body in the Bag Murder.' Inside the bag that contained the head was a blood soaked T-shirt, and an ominous sign for those involved in the murder hunt was that the shirt was of the type that was issued to prisoners on their discharge from prison.

Forensics had by this time established the manufacturer of the bags in which the 'packages' had been found. One had been made in Taiwan, and had not been on general sale in the United Kingdom, but rather had been predominantly distributed in New Zealand and Australia. Further expert examination also revealed that the man's jaw bone was not thought to be 'European in type.' This fact tallied with the assumption that, because of the large number of moles on the dead man's body, he was a native of the southern hemisphere, where solar radiation was greater and would therefore account for the extra quantity of the moles.

With this in mind and armed with the computer-generated photograph of the murder victim the police contacted their counterparts in both the Australian and New Zealand police forces. Extensive media coverage was given to the Gwent police inquiry in both countries, as well as in the South Wales area. Within hours of the broadcasts the victim's name finally became known: he was Clive Tully. It was a former workmate who was able to make the positive identification. Tully had been on holiday in the United Kingdom and shortly before his murder had visited relatives in the Newport area.[11] Police checks were made, and it was established that the victim was known to have been in Bristol only two days prior to his mutilated body being found at Rogerstone. Having traced Clive's address, police rushed to a converted house in which Tully's flat was situated. Fingerprints and personal possessions found within the flat confirmed that this had indeed been the victim's home. A search was made in the adjacent flats: and in that of Malcolm Green, a heavily-bloodstained carpet was found concealed under a bed. Information now led the police to the home of Green's girlfriend, Helen Barnes,[12] the twenty-two-year-old daughter of a vicar. Police surveillance was kept on the girl's address and some time later Helen, accompanied by her parents and Green, arrived home having apparently been out for a meal. Green was arrested.

Events were now moving rapidly and confirmation that the Body in the Bag was indeed Clive Tully came from the New Zealand police who had checked on Clive's dental records. From the discovery of the bags to the arrest of Green the investigation had taken only ten days. Throughout his trial, which was held in Bristol, Malcolm John Green, a 43-year-old builder of Luxton Street, in the Easton area of the city, maintained his innocence. But his innocence was always in doubt. The evidence against Green was overwhelming, an eye witness pointed out Green at an identification parade as the man he had seen taking bags out of a white Metro car and driving off leaving the baggage behind. Helen Barnes who owned the Metro had loaned the car to Green on the day that the bags had been found. This plus the blood-soaked carpet in Green's flat, clearly indicated his guilt. But any uncertainty was beyond question when it was revealed that Green had already served 18 years for a murder he had committed in 1971.[13] Described as a psychopath[14]

Jail penalty: 'Fifteen will stay locked up'

Body-in-bags murderer 'will never be freed'

27 FEB 1995

By Amanda Evans

BODY-in-bags murderer Malcolm Green, whose story shocked the people of Gwent, is one of 15 inmates who have been told they will never be re-leased from jail, it has been claimed.

The 47-year-old was sentenced in October 1991 to a minimum of 25 years for the murder of New Zealand visitor Clive Tully.

The dismembered body of Mr Tully was found parcelled up in a lay-by at Rogerstone. His head and hands were found two miles away.

Green had previously

MALCOLM GREEN: Will spend life in jail

CLIVE TULLY: The New Zealand visitor who was his victim

"whole life" tariff on them.

A "tariff" is set on

a whole-life tariff.

The Observer compiled the list of names after

Others who have been told they will never be released include Moors murderer Myra Hindley and serial killer Dennis Nilsen, called the Black Panther, who killed three subpostmasters during robberies.

He also kidnapped the heiress Lesley Whittle and left her tied up.

Malcolm Green, the man convicted for the Body-in-the-Bag murder.

Green had slashed his first victim to death using a broken glass, and had only been released from prison five months before he murdered Tully. Throughout his time in prison he had become known as a troublemaker and accordingly was frequently transferred from prison to prison. During his final years behind bars Green had studied 'A' Level Human Biology on a day-release course at Filton Technical College. It was this understanding of the human body gained on the course, plus the fact that he had once worked in a slaughterhouse that led one expert to comment, 'that it was his knowledge of human anatomy which enabled him to make such a neat job of butchering tragic Clive Tully.' Green was sentenced to serve a minimum of twenty-five years, thus ending the murder investigation that was described as being 'one of the most horrific ever known in Wales.'

Following the trial Green made an appeal against the sentence claiming the findings were 'unsafe and unsatisfactory,' but his application was dismissed. The three judges of the Appeal Court upheld the sentence, and Lord Justice Simon Brown commented that 'The evidence was ample to support this conviction. In reality the evidence was overwhelming. None of us feels a lurking doubt over the safety of this conviction.' In 1995 Green was informed by the then Home Secretary, Michael Howard, that he would never be released from gaol. The callous murderer was one of 15 prisoners who would never be eligible for parole, because of the 'whole life tariff' imposed on them.[15] Green found himself in the infamous company of some of the country's most evil killers, amongst whom were counted Myra Hindley, the Moors murderer, and the serial killer Dennis Nilsen.

April 22nd, 1994.

The Risca Taxi Murders:

Gerald Stevens and Christine Rees

The arrival of several pornographic photographs through the letter boxes of Gerry Stevens and Christine Rees was a prelude to one of Gwent's most horrific double murders of the 20th Century. That fateful date was April 22nd, 1994. The photos crudely showed both Stevens and Rees in explicit sexual poses. As both were married, the appearance of the unannounced packages boded ill for the recipients. The sender of the photographs had obviously intended to cause great embarrassment to the couple's spouses. Little did they realise that this was the opening gambit in a game that would eventually lead to murder. Gerald Stevens, a joint-partner in a local taxi firm trading as Western Valley Taxis, was married, and a father of three children. Christine Rees, who drove a taxi for the company, was also married and was the mother of four children. From the very outset Stevens and Rees formed a close relationship, and before long they had become lovers. Their association was soon common knowledge in the small valley community of Risca. The pair did little to hide their affection towards each another and this lack of discretion was to prove a major factor in the tragedy that was to follow. Soon tragedy would unfold and uncover a story of lust, jealousy, greed and revenge. It was inevitable, amongst such high passions, that the story of the tangled relationships and of family feuds would be exposed.

In the early hours of May 6th, a frantic 999 call brought police rushing to the offices of the Western Valley Taxi firm situated on the Birds Industrial Estate, Risca. They were responding to a phone call from a shocked taxi driver who had discovered two bodies lying in the firm's office. The arrival of the police confirmed the man's worst fears; the pair were dead, having apparently been violently beaten and then shot. The victims had been murdered in what was described by Detective Superintendent Bennett of the Gwent C.I.D. as being 'a particularly nasty attack'. The victims were named as 42-year-old Gerry Stevens, a part-owner of the business, and one of the firm's taxi drivers, 37-year-old Christine Rees. Because of the ferocity of the assault on both the victims the police suspected a 'crime of passion' and there could be little doubt that the double murder was a cold-blooded attempt by the killer to hide his identity by silencing his victims.

Within a few hours of the grim discovery armed police raided a house on a local housing estate. Startled neighbours, many roused from their sleep, were shocked at the drama being enacted outside their bedroom windows. One of those disturbed was Andrew Elias, an insurance salesman, who later told a reporter that 'It was like something on television', adding that 'there were about ten officers involved, hiding behind walls.' Shortly afterwards, onlookers saw a man, later identified as Paul Rees, the husband of one of the murder victims, being escorted by the police from the house and driven away. Within a few minutes the area was deserted, the only evidence that anything untoward had occurred was the solitary policeman left to guard the house. A similar raid was made on the home of Stevens's eldest son, Andrew, who was also taken into custody. Later that day amid the comings and goings at the crime scene, the other business partner in the taxi firm, Michael Attwooll, accompanied police to the offices to identify records that might be required in the investigation.

As news of the murders spread, the full impact that the slayings were to have on the friends and families of both victims soon became apparent. Besides the widow and widower who had lost their respective partners there were also seven children who had lost one of their parents. The close-knit communities of Risca and Pontywaun were horrified at the slayings. Neighbours were quick to relate how the two deaths had cast a gloom over the whole area. There was little doubt that both victims had been good neighbours, although here and there the whisperers told of 'carryings-on' within the taxi firm that was best not spoken of. Through local newspapers and television broadcasts, appeals were made to the public, and in particular to anyone who had used the taxi service the previous night. Preliminary examinations of the bodies revealed that a weapon such as a machete or meat cleaver had been the probable weapon used in the ferocious and sustained attack on the couple. Wounds to the hands and arms of Mrs Rees showed that she had tried desperately to fight off her assailant. Mr Stevens was found dead in his seat. After suffering the horrendous slashing injuries both the victims had been shot through the head at point blank range. This attack had, according to a police spokesman, all the markings of a 'contract killing'.

Throughout the length and breadth of the valley rumours spread like wildfire. Those who had been the whisperers the day before, now openly claimed to be 'in the know'. They told everyone who would listen that the police were investigating the existence of photographs showing a depraved Gerry Stevens dressed in women's underwear. A copy of the photos had, they said, been sent to the partners of both Stevens and Rees. Many others claimed to have known that both of the victims had been cheating on their respective spouses and that the couple had had a love nest somewhere in the town.

Early results of the post mortem indicated that the fatal shots had been fired by a .22 calibre weapon, and that both the deceased had extensive injuries to their hands, neck and face. Again the police appealed for any witnesses to come forward. Whoever had committed the crime, they said, would have been spattered with the blood of the two victims. Later that evening, after being kept in custody overnight, Paul Rees and Andrew Stevens who had been taken into custody the day previous, and were said to be 'helping the police with their inquiries', were released without charges being made against them.

The next morning Monday, May 9th, a press conference was scheduled for 10am. However, prior to the meeting, the arrival at the police station of Vincent Price, Attwooll's brother-in-law, saw a new flurry of activity. Price informed the police that he had sold Attwooll 'a converted air rifle, one that was capable of firing .22 bullets that would mushroom on impact.' Having purchased the gun in 1993 'as a novelty, although knowing it to be illegal', he had later sold it to his brother-in-law for £100. The gun came complete with a silencer and two boxes of ammunition, each containing about fifty bullets. On the day of the murders, he told the detectives, Attwooll had called at his house and had asked him how he could get the 'Nitro'[16] off his hands. Price suggested that he use bleach, which he did – washing his hands in Price's kitchen. After Attwooll left, he had become suspicious of his brother-in-law's involvement with the murders and had decided to report the conversation to the police. Acting on the information supplied by Price, Michael Attwooll was arrested.

With only minutes to spare before the press conference a police spokesman told the waiting news reporters of the dramatic new developments in the case. In a statement they told the press that they had arrested a fifty-year-old local man in connection with the double murder, and were 'not looking for anyone else in connection to the investigation'. They also indicated that another line of inquiry was being undertaken, that a possible motive for the murders could be a grudge connection within the taxi business itself. Furthermore it appeared that another employee of the taxi firm had been attacked some weeks before the murders. The unnamed man had been slashed with a knife receiving wounds to his thigh and shoulder before his assailants had run off. An additional disclosure at the conference was the discovery of the love nest shared by the victims, a flat in Channel View Court, Risca. The tenant of the flat was Vicky Attwooll, Michael Attwooll's daughter. Also sharing the flat was John Roden, Vicky's boyfriend. From information gathered it was believed that the couple's illicit affair had began early in 1994 when they started to meet at the flat regularly for sex. Stevens paid Roden for the use of their trysting place. However, during their visit to the flat, the police discovered cannabis plants growing in the couple's kitchen and a further search uncovered two wraps of the drug amphetamine. As a result of this discovery they arrested John Roden, and he was taken to the police station and questioned about the illegal drugs found on the premises. He was later charged with possession.

Michael Thomas Attwooll appeared before the Tredegar magistrates and was remanded in custody at Cardiff Prison for seven days. Yet despite this arrest, the weapons, thought to be a meat cleaver and a .22 rifle, had not yet been recovered. At this stage of the investigation forty police officers continued their house-to-house inquiries; meanwhile a thorough search was being made for the murder weapons.

A rival Risca taxi firm's rather callous attitude when they sought to take over the Western Valley Taxis business shocked many in the local community. Their bid came only days after the double killing had occurred. Sonia Bird who was responsible for the management of the industrial site on which the Western Valley Taxis had their offices said, 'I have had an inquiry from JB Taxis as well as two other local firms . . . but JB were specifically asking for the Western Valley site'. She continued, 'I have never dealt with anything like this before . . . I will have to speak to the police and Mr Attwooll's solicitor.' When contacted by the local press about the speed of their approach to Sonia Bird in connection with the takeover of the taxis firm's offices, they sensibly declined to comment.

On May 12th Attwooll was again brought before Tredegar Magistrates where he was charged with the double murder, and was returned to Cardiff Prison.

The inquest was held at Newport on May 16th. The Coroner, Mr David Bowen, read extracts from the post-mortem report provided by Professor Bernard Knight concerning the nature of the injuries and the causes of death. Mr Stevens died as the result of two gunshot wounds to the head. He had also suffered slash wounds to his face and head. Mrs Rees's death was also the result of a similar gunshot wound, and like Stevens she had also been the victim of a vicious attack, receiving eleven slash wounds from a heavy bladed weapon now thought to be a machete. The wounds were inflicted to her scalp, cheek, ear and neck. All the bullet wounds showed smoke scorching, this being consistent with shots being discharged at very close range. Having read out the report the Coroner then adjourned his court until January 13th, 1996.

Gerry Stevens was buried on May 19th. The emotional service was held at St John's Church, Cwmcarn. It was a beautiful summer's day, one that belied the solemnity of the occasion. Inside the small village church two hundred friends and relatives packed the pews while a further thirty or more stood in silence outside. To add to the fervour of the service, hymns were sung by the Risca Male Voice Choir. Their voices filled the small church with a passion and sadness that only Welsh singing could bring. The local community had buried one of its own, and the whole valley mourned.

New evidence as to Attwooll's guilt came from an unlikely source when, in June, a remand prisoner at Cardiff Prison, David Eaves, contacted the police and made a statement to them. He told detectives that while sharing a cell Attwooll had been boasting to Eaves and other fellow inmates about carrying out the murders. In fact Attwooll's boasting had amounted to what could only be described as 'a full and detailed confession to the committing of the murders.'

On June 22nd John Roden was brought before the magistrates on drug-related charges. He admitted to possession of the drugs found at the flat he shared with Vicky Attwooll, and was fined £200. In August a gun was recovered from the River Ebbw: it had been burnt and dismantled before being thrown into the water. It was later identified by Vincent Price as probably being the gun he had sold to Attwooll. Further inquiries led police to the home of Carl Perkins, who lived at Tan-y-Bryn. Perkins, a friend of Roden, told the police that he had often visited Attwooll's daughter, Vicky, to buy cannabis from her. However, when she had been caught by the police, he then obtained the drug from Roden with whom Vicky was living. Perkins continued that Roden had asked him to dispose of a black bag containing two parts of a gun that had been burnt. Furthermore he had been offered a share in £300 if he helped him (Roden) to put two cars out of action although he hadn't said which cars. Later he had been shown some 'dirty photographs' and was asked to deliver them for an additional £30. When questioned about a conversation he had had with Roden sometime prior to the murders, Perkins said, 'Roden told me that Mike had a gun . . . and that they were going to go and shoot Gerry and Christine.' As Perkins's garden backed onto the River Ebbw, he had thrown the gun into the water behind his house where it had been recovered by the police sometime in August, a few months after the killings. He had also been asked by Roden to look after a bloodstained belt while the latter had gone to the police station. Following Perkins's disclosure, the police arrested Roden and he was charged with the dual killing.

The trial, due to begin on May 2nd, 1996, was delayed owing to legal submissions. Having sworn in the jury the trial was postponed until the following day. However when the trial finally started, Roger Thomas QC appeared for the prosecution. He described the killings as 'brutal and particularly savage that were planned, deliberate and ruthless'. It had been Attwooll who had arranged for the photographs of the murdered couple to be sent to their respective partners. The photographs had been found in the office by one of the firm's taxi drivers, Anthony Osmunde. Osmunde known locally as 'Ozy' had later handed the photographs to Vicky Attwooll, with whom he had once had a relationship. Osmunde failed to turn up in court for the trial. Fears were expressed as to whether he had been threatened, and told not to appear. The judge issued a warrant for his arrest as it was believed that the missing witness had absconded to the north of England.[17] However in a statement to the police earlier, 'Ozy' had told them that 'The photos were depicting Mrs Rees and Mr Stevens performing explicit sexual acts.' They had been sent to Stevens's wife and Rees's husband a week before the murders had taken place. Paul Rees, Christine's husband denied any knowledge of the photographs or of the affair between Stevens and his wife. Further revelations indicated that Attwooll believed that his partner was cheating him by 'skimming off' a percentage of the fares. He was also heard describing Stevens as a 'dirty, kinky bastard', and saying that Mrs Rees was 'a lazy bastard.' Gerry Stevens was known to be a lady's man, having at one time, it was revealed, had a wife and two mistresses. But it was his affair with Christine Rees that had caused great resentment amongst most of the taxi firm's employees.

Called to the witness stand Vicky Attwooll told the court that on the night of the murders her father had called at her home, which she shared with Roden, who was also accused of the killings. The time, she claimed, was between 12.30am and 12.35am. She remembered the time distinctly, as she recalled that she was winding her alarm clock at the time of his visit. When asked if she had 'spiced up her evidence' to provide her father with an alibi, she denied the claim. But she did admit under questioning that she had been instrumental in sending the pornographic photographs to the victims' spouses.

Evidence was presented before the court of the relationship between the two murder victims. It was common knowledge throughout the community that both were lovers. Employees of the taxi firm told of them openly 'kissing and cuddling' while in the office. Throughout the trial the jury heard a constant stream of damning evidence against the two accused. Neighbours of the taxi office told of raised voices being heard, followed by a loud bang. Forensic evidence revealed that blood samples taken from Attwooll's car matched the blood types of both Stevens and Rees. The witnesses all told of the irrefutable links between the accused and the murdered couple.

A second prisoner from Cardiff gaol also gave evidence against both the defendants. The prisoner, Geoffrey Woodland, told the court that when told of the murders by the accused (Attwooll) he thought that he was lying. It was, he said, 'what sounded like something out of James Bond, and I didn't believe it at first'. Previously he had told the police that he had been told by the accused how and where the weapons had been disposed of shortly after the murders had been committed. All the evidence presented before the court was a damning indictment of the guilt of Attwooll and his henchman Roden. At the close of the trial the judge urged the twelve members of the jury, consisting of seven women and five men, not to be 'swayed by their emotions at the brutality of the crime.' He added, 'We can feel horror and outrage at what happened . . . But none of these emotions will give you the slightest help in deciding whether the defendants are guilty or not.' At that point the jury retired to decide the fate of the two men who stood accused of the vicious murders. By mid-afternoon both counsels were called back into the courtroom, the jury had requested clarification on certain points in the evidence given by one of the witnesses. As the first day of their deliberations came to a close there had been no progress in reaching a verdict. The second day likewise saw no movement by the members of the jury. And it was later on the third day of their retirement that they finally reached a verdict. The three days waiting for news of the findings had proved particularly fraught for the families of both the accused and their alleged victims. With their return to the courtroom both Attwooll and Roden stared impassively as their fate was announced, in a clear voice the foreman read out, 'Guilty'. As the judge Mr Justice Jowitt, passed the sentences of life imprisonment on each of the men there was no outward sign of emotion from either of the two killers. In his concluding remarks the judge told the two standing in the dock, 'These were cold-blooded, vicious and brutal crimes.' He continued, 'It is quite clear from the photographs that the jury and I have had to see that the butchery practised upon Christine Rees was quite appalling. It was said by one witness that she put up fight and paid dearly for it, and now so must both of you.' Quietly the callous killers were led away. The lives of the murder victims' families had been put on hold for a year. For the two who were now being escorted from the court, their lives would be put on hold for a very long time to come. Attwooll began serving his twenty-year sentence as an inmate of Gartree prison in Leicestershire, while Roden, who had been moved from Cardiff Prison to Wormwood Scrubs, had been informed that he would have to serve at least 18 years of his life sentence.

In September 1995, Roden's family claimed that there had been a miscarriage of justice during the trial, on the grounds that the evidence of one of the principal witnesses against Roden, Carl Perkins, was unsafe. Roden's sister, Gillian Edwards, told reporters that they were hoping to uncover fresh evidence that would exonerate her brother of the crime. Within days of Roden's call for a mis-trial, Attwooll also sought permission to gain leave of appeal against his conviction. He lodged a complaint against one of the detectives who had been a member of the Crime Team that had brought the two killers to justice. However in May 1996 his complaints were dismissed and both men's leave of appeals were rejected.

However that was not the end of the story, for Roden's family vowed to fight on for the release of the prisoners. A campaign has been mounted to protest the innocence of the convicted killers. Following the dismissal of their appeals, Roden's family and friends have maintained a high public profile by carrying on a crusade against his conviction. Mary Roden, his mother, has fought tirelessly to draw attention to her son's plight, steadfastly maintaining his innocence. They hope to clear both Attwooll's and Roden's names and have their sentences quashed. In February 1998 fresh hopes were raised when a government agency, the Criminal Cases Review Commission, agreed to re-examine the evidence presented at the trial to see if there were grounds for an appeal. This was bolstered by the claim that new evidence had come to light, mainly that most of the machete wounds inflicted on Christine Rees had been on the right side of her body – suggesting that the killer who had wielded the weapon had been left-handed, and it was pointed out that both Attwooll and Roden were right-handed. In September 1999 Attwooll gave an interview to a reporter of the *South Wales Argus* from his prison cell denying any involvement in the murders. Shortly after Christmas a candlelight vigil was held in John Frost Square, Newport, in an additional effort to highlight the campaign. A further vigil was held in August 2000, when Mary Roden and her family made a protest on the steps of Newport Crown Court as well as outside the Welsh Assembly at Cardiff. The latter was to coincide with Roden's thirty-fifth birthday. The tactics proved successful for they gained support from Mr Griffith, The Welsh Assembly Member for Newport East, to petition the Home Secretary, Jack Straw, 'in an effort to secure an appeal.' This support however did not succeed in bringing about a decision to refer the case to a review panel, and in April 2001 Roden's family were still campaigning unsuccessfully.

Whether or not Attwooll and Roden are indeed guilty of the murders they were convicted of is for the legal system to determine. But for Mary Roden, her son's innocence is beyond doubt for Mary took an unusual and perhaps controversial step when she sought the help of a clairvoyant. The woman, who did not want to be identified for fear of reprisals, hoped through her physic powers to locate the still missing machete used in the double murder. She told Mary that 'your son didn't do it.' The medium offered an alternative scenario of the brutal crime: her theory as to the real identity and motivation of the murderers was, she said, 'Three men . . . who visited the taxi office, cold and callous killers, yet excited by their murderous spree and fuelled by drugs.' Is it possible that the real truth of the Risca Taxi Murders lies not in the findings of the cold science of forensic evidence, but rather can only be found in a psychic message from beyond the grave?

May 11th, 1996

The Death of a Small Time Gangster:

Tyrone France

Reports of a large fire in Wentwood Forest brought two forestry workers to a clearing above the small village of Parc Seymour close to the main A48 Newport to Chepstow road. The fire was sited away from the numerous footpaths that criss-crossed this popular, wooded camping area of Gwent. The two men sent to investigate the blaze came upon the spent remnants of a large fire. The few wisps of smoke rising from the heap of smouldering embers carried with it into the still night air the sickeningly pungent odour of burning flesh. On raking through the ashes they made a grisly discovery, for there, amongst the glowing mound were several charred and flame-blackened bones. And at the edge of the dying fire was the gruesome spectacle of a human foot. Police appealed for any information as to the identity of the victim.

News of the horrific discovery filled the headlines of the local newspaper, the *South Wales Argus*. The paper's headlines told of the 'FOREST MURDER RIDDLE', and briefly outlined the discovery of the body. Initially it was thought to be impossible to determine the age or sex of the victim. This was due partly to the fact that the remains were incomplete, the torso not being found in or at the scene of the fire, and the ferocity of the flames having reduced much of the body to ash. It was estimated that the body had been burning approximately three to four hours before its discovery. Immediately, wild rumours spread around the locality that the death and subsequent burning of the body was possibly linked to witchcraft and human sacrifice. Witch covens were once known to be active in this area.

The macabre task of trying to establish the identity of the murder victim fell to Mr Rick James, a Home Office pathologist. However, using the measurements of the human foot as well as the bones recovered from the site, James was able to establish that the person, a male, would have stood a little over six foot tall. The age of the victim was estimated to be in his late teens or mid-twenties. To further assist in identifying the unknown man, Dr David Wittaker a dental expert, who had been involved in the notorious Fred and Rose West murders, examined some of the thirteen teeth that had been found amongst the ashes of the fire. Forensic scientists began DNA testing to further the police efforts in identifying the victim.

Photographs of partially-burnt clothing and other personal effects recovered from the flames appeared in the local newspaper with the hope that someone, somewhere, would recognise them. The heavily-charred clothing consisted of a denim jacket, a lumberjack-type overcoat and two shirts, one of which bore the words 'Reggae and Red Stripe.' Among the personal items found was a Citizen watch, its hands having stopped at one o'clock, and several small metallic ornaments each of a highly-distinctive nature, and four door keys. It was these items that finally led to the identification of the victim four days after the grim discovery in the secluded woodland glade.

The police confirmed that the body of the murder victim was that of Tyrone Jason France, a person well known to the Gwent Police. Indeed France, prior to his death, had been on police bail in connection with an armed robbery. He had been arrested on suspicion of robbing the Royal Oak sub-post office on the outskirts of Newport of £6,000. The post office had been raided in March 1996, and the raid allegedly had been carried out by France and an unnamed accomplice. The Magistrates' hearing into the robbery was to have taken place on May 29th. Much speculation arose from the suggestion that France, who sometimes used the aliases of Williams, Harris, Holmes and Francis, had committed the robbery to fund an illegal drugs deal. If this were true then such a large purchase would have undoubtedly catapulted France into the premier league of drug dealers in the South Wales area, but such a move would have brought him into direct confrontation with other established local drug dealers. Detective Superintendent Ian Johnson, who led the investigation, commented that 'one part of our inquiry is the suggestion that somebody thinks he was a police informer' – a belief that was shared by many in the local criminal fraternity.

Police assumed that France had been murdered in the forest clearing where the body had been incinerated, and a number of local people were thought to have been involved in the crime. On May 16th, news broke of two arrests being made in connection with the murder of Tyrone France. The suspects were 23-year-old Simon Spring of Ringland, Newport and Dylan Watcyns, aged 21, who lived in the St Julians area of the town. A third suspect, an unnamed youth had by the next day also been taken to Newport Central Police Station. Two further arrests in connection with the murder saw the arrival at the Central Police Station of a married couple, 39-year-old David Dominy and his wife Helen. Both had been arrested and charged with 'taking possession of and concealing a firearm and ammunition, with intent to impede the apprehension or the prosecution of Simon Spring.' Like Spring, the Dominys were from Beatty Road on the Ringland housing estate of Newport. The couple were granted bail, a condition of which was that they should not interfere with any of the prosecution witnesses.

On May 20th, the unnamed youth who had been helping the police with their enquiries appeared before the town magistrates, charged with the murder of France. He was named as Jason Preece who lived at Lower Dock Street, Newport. Preece who remained silent throughout the hearing was described as a Gulf War veteran. He was remanded in custody and was led away to join Spring and Watcyns who were already on remand.

Following these arrests the police felt confident enough to release further details of Tyrone's murder. He had been shot with a 9mm handgun. A spent cartridge and a 9mm bullet were found close to the fire, indicating that the victim had, as they had suspected, been shot in the clearing. After his death, his body had been doused with petrol that had then been set alight. The murder, they said, had all the indications of having been carried out in what seemed to be an execution-style killing. The next day the missing torso of Tyrone France was found on the muddy banks of the River Usk at Caerleon. It was taken away for forensic testing to determine its identity. The three men arrested by the police were then formally charged with the murder of France.

The trial began on January 15th, 1997, at Newport Crown Court. And from the outset it was to be plagued with numerous delays. Before it actually started, the trial had to be postponed when Mr Justice Curtis, the trial judge, injured himself while skiing. He had suffered a dislocated collarbone. On the first day of the hearing there was an immediate delay owing to legal arguments made by both the defence and prosecution counsels. These were heard by the judge and the trial was adjourned until the following day.

Once the trial was underway, the sordid business of the slaying began to unfold. The jury heard that Tyrone France had been a 'small time drugs dealer and gangster', and that he had been lured to the Wentwood Forest by Watcyns, Spring and Preece, the three men responsible for his death, each of whom he had considered to be his friend. France had been shot in the head and set alight after a can of petrol was poured over his body. Having murdered their victim the three defendants had driven off in a car. However, some time later that same evening the group had returned to the scene of their crime and discovered that the trunk of the body had not been destroyed. In a desperate bid to dispose of the un-burnt portion of the corpse, they removed the torso from the fire and placed it into the boot of the car. Then the three accomplices drove six miles or so to the picturesque village of Caerleon, where on an isolated section of the Bulmore Road they dumped the partly-burnt body into the river. The Counsel for the Prosecution claimed that Spring, Watcyns and Preece had planned and carried out the cold-blooded murder of 26-year-old Tyrone France. It was disclosed that Watcyns and Spring had travelled to the forest clearing on the morning prior to the fatal shooting in order to collect and stack timber ready to be used in the disposal of their intended victim. The Prosecution also claimed that it was both Spring and Watcyns who had planned and carried out the cold-blooded murder; and that they had shot their victim in cold blood. The bullet entered the chest, before passing through the heart and finally lodging itself in the right lung. This, according to the pathologist who had performed the autopsy, was the shot that had killed France. It had been fired from a distance of about ten metres. A second bullet had then been shot into the corpse at close range as it lay upon the grass. The court was adjourned so that the jury could be taken to Wentwood Forest to see for themselves the woodland glade where the crime had been committed.

Throughout the proceedings all three defendants denied their guilt, although Spring admitted to the lesser charge of manslaughter on the grounds of diminished responsibility. Watcyns and Preece also denied that they had tried to pervert the course of justice by assisting in the disposal and concealment of evidence relating to the killing. There was little doubt that the murder was premeditated, as the wood intended to cremate the body had been piled on top of the corpse before being set alight. It had, as the court had heard, been carefully collected and stacked some hours earlier that day.

The defence counsel claimed that Spring had murdered France because the small-time drugs dealer had had him stalked some months earlier. Furthermore, Spring claimed that France had tried to have him killed some time prior to the murder. Confusion was added to the case when Spring's accomplices, Watcyns and Preece, told police that the victim was killed because Spring had told them that he wanted to get his own back because France had assaulted his girlfriend and her child.

The numerous delays continued while counsel argued on points of law, and the admission of fresh evidence. For two days Michelle Rogers, the girlfriend of Jason Preece, gave evidence. Under cross examination she told the court that some weeks before the murder, Preece had told her that he would do 'six to eight years for Tyrone'. It was pointed out to the jury that Miss Rogers had lied to the police, claiming that Preece had been with her on the night of the murder at a local night club called TJ's. It was suggested that her testimony might therefore be unreliable. As her testimony came to an end Miss Rogers broke down in a flood of tears and the trial was once more brought to a halt.

As the case proceeded lurid allegations were made that France was a victim of a contract killing. David Aubrey Q.C. told the court that Joanne Jones, Simon Spring's girlfriend, had taken out a 'contract' on France for his murder. He claimed that at the age of fourteen, Joanne Jones was involved with the murder victim. During their relationship she had been severely beaten by him, the resulting injuries were such that Miss Jones would require medication for the rest of her life.

Preece, who had already admitted to the lesser charge of manslaughter through diminished reasonability, claimed to be suffering

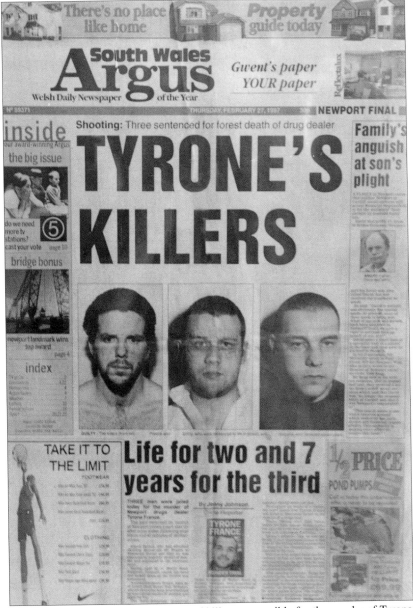

Newspaper headlines showing the trio of killers responsible for the murder of Tyrone France, a small time gangster.

from a psychiatric disorder, notably Post Traumatic Stress, and Gulf War Syndrome. These health problems had, argued Preece's counsel, made the defendant vulnerable to the influences of someone with a stronger personality. And so the case dragged on. Again delays beset the trial when one of the jurors became ill. Finally, after six long weeks of sifting through the evidence presented before the court, the jury retired to consider their verdict. After nine hours and forty-five minutes they returned to the courtroom. All three men accused of the callous murder of France were found Guilty.

A majority verdict saw Spring sentenced to life imprisonment. Jason Preece, who had set fire to the victim's body, also received a life sentence. Dylan Watcyns, was acquitted of murder, but given a seven-year sentence for manslaughter.

MONMOUTHSHIRE MISCELLANY

The Houses of Correction

They Plied Their Deadly Trade in Gwent

The Penny Dreadful

Monmouthshire's Houses of Correction:

Monmouth Prison

There have been two gaols in Gwent, the first one to be built was constructed at Monmouth, and was completed in 1790. The other prison built at Usk, which was later to replace its predecessor at Monmouth, was opened in 1843. There is a scarcity of illustrations of the old Monmouth Prison, but from the frugal sources available its description speaks of 'a massive building, looking more like a castle than a gaol, having high outer walls, and an inner building complete with a tall round bastion'. We know that it cost £5,000 to build and was constructed of local stone, some 18,000 tons being removed from a quarry situated in Lower Redbrook. The building was located on the Hereford Road, overlooking the town from the area aptly named Hangman's Hill.[18] John Fentiman Newington Butts, a builder from Surrey, constructed the gaol. It was intended from the outset that to ensure the disciplining of the prisoners, hard labour was to be employed at the prison, as well as the administering of corporal punishment. The term 'hard labour' was interpreted as 'useful employment'. In the first few decades of the 19th Century to ensure that prisoners were usefully employed a treadmill was installed within the prison walls. The use of the treadmills in prisons was according to some the perpetual symbol of all that was wrong with the early penal policy of British justice. It had been devised in 1818 by an English civil engineer.[19] And its principle use was solely to solve the problem of providing a means of employing the large and mainly idle prison population found within British gaols.

His idea was largely based on the 'horse gins', huge wheels that were driven by domesticated animals. Sir William adapted this traditional design, itself an adaptation of the more ancient devices that had been used to grind corn or raise water since biblical times.

Brixton Prison was the first prison to have the treadmill installed and for many years it proved to be a popular attraction as members of the public were allowed to watch the spectacle of the inmates at work.

These huge devices were operated by the convicts with the same movement as climbing stairs, and they usually accommodated upwards of ten prisoners.

In their report on the 'Criminal Prisons of London' (1862), authors Mayhew and Binney gave a contemporary description of the treadmill:

> Each wheel contains twenty-four steps which are eight inches apart, so that the circumference of the cylinder is sixteen feet. The wheels revolve twice in one minute, and the mechanism is arranged to ring a bell at the end of every thirtieth revolution, and so announce that the appointed spell of work is finished. Every man put to labour at the wheel has to work for fifteen quarters of an hour every day.
>
> The prisoners call the occupation 'grinding the wind'; and that is really the only description applicable to it – the sole object of the labour of some 150 men, employed for eight hours per day, being simply to put in motion a big fan, or regulator, as it is called, which, impinging on the air as it revolves, serves to add to the severity of the work by increasing the resistance.

In time this utterly pointless means of keeping prisoners 'busy' was given some purpose by attaching the wheel to some grinding or pumping mechanism so that the energy created at least had some beneficial effect.

Treadmills had mostly been abandoned by the early twentieth century, and of the 39 still in operation in 1895 only thirteen survived into the new century. The health of the prisoners was of paramount concern and no inmate could be put to work on the treadmill without the consent of a surgeon. The permitted time that could be allocated to any male convict was a maximum of 12,000 feet (treads on the wheel).

The first Governor of the Monmouth Prison was Mr James Baker who received the princely sum of £100 per annum. Holding such a position, one would imagine, required many skills. Certainly the Governor was responsible for the both the physical and spiritual welfare of the inmates as well as the day-to-day running of such an establishment in a way that the holder of the office would be held above reproach. But several of the Governors gained notoriety, records showing that drunkenness was a major source of complaint. Indeed the Gaol's governor in 1841, a Mr

Monmouth Gaol prior to its demolition in the 19th century.

The Old Monmouth County Gaol gatehouse, on the old Hereford Road.

Ford, was discharged from his position for being repeatedly absent from his post. It was noted that he often returned to the prison late at night in a continual state of intoxication. A new governor, Mr Samuel Barrett, was duly appointed, being selected for his prior knowledge and experience as Assistant Governor of Bristol Gaol. Barrett remained governor of the prison for twelve years until 1854, when he was arrested and put on trial at Usk for issuing a forged receipt for the value of £8.13.11d to the County Treasurer. Further charges were brought against him for the felonious utterance of receipts to the total value of £80.6.8d. At his trial evidence was presented to the court that during his governorship of the prison he had spent in excess of £900 of his own money on improvements to the prison. This had little effect on the court and Barrett was sentenced to fifteen years' transportation. He was fifty-five years old. His goods were seized and sold to defray his debts and his wife was evicted from their quarters within the prison.

USK PRISON

During 1839 a committee was set up to establish the viability and the costs involved in the building of a new House of Correction at Usk. The budget, it was stipulated, was not to exceed £16,000. The criteria for location for the new building were threefold: firstly it was to eventually replace the old County Gaol at Monmouth. Monmouth was too far removed from the growing and riotous mining communities of the eastern and western valleys to enable the quick transportation of prisoners. Secondly it was to replace the old and deteriorated existing House of Correction then situated in Bridge Street, Usk, and thirdly it was to provide a more modern building that was to be designed on the recently completed model prison at Pentonville. By the middle of the following year plans were in hand for the work to begin on the new structure. Thomas Wyatt, president of the Royal Institute of British Architects, was appointed as the architect responsible for drawing up the plans. Finally permission was granted, and work commenced on the new prison that was designed to hold one hundred and fifty male, and fifty female prisoners. These inmates were to be kept 'silent and separate'[20] a system much favoured by the early Victorians. A report dated July 29th, 1843 establishes that prisoners were being incarcerated within the prison. In 1869 Usk became the County Gaol, and the old prison at Monmouth was demolished shortly afterwards, and eight years later the gaol became the responsibility of the newly formed Prison Commission. The prison has had a varied history since it was built more than 155 years ago. It had, for a short period in its history, housed both men and women inmates. While the men were required to perform hard manual labour by breaking large rocks brought to the jail from local quarries. Women prisoners were put to work at Oakum Picking, a boring and painful task untwisting the remnants of sisal ropes. The residue of the ropes was used as mattress-filling, for making mats,[21] or, when mixed with tar, as caulking for the wooden hulled ships. Like its predecessor at Monmouth, Usk had its own Tread Wheel installed. In January 1887, the Secretary of State to the Home Office issued the following directive to Usk Prison, 'That the 1st Class Labour should consist of Stone-breaking and Tread Wheel as heretofore, with this exception in detail as to the Tread wheel, that now the wheel is to be kept constantly in motion, each man working for 15 minutes, and resting for 5 minutes, whereas under the old system the prisoners worked *together* for 10 minutes: and rested *together* for 10 minutes.'

The infamous wheel remained in use at Usk until 1901 when it appears to have been finally abandoned. Following its dismantling this Victorian punitive symbol of wasted effort was buried beneath what is now the prison's sports field.

In 1922 the prison was closed for a short period before being utilised as a Borstal to house young offenders. A proposal to build a specialist Borstal unit at Abergavenny, near the Lanover Estate brought an immediate protest from Lord Lanover, who made it clear that having such a criminal element almost on his doorstep was unacceptable. Hastily the plans were dropped and the unit was later built at Little Mill, a typical case of 'Nimby'.[22] Usk once more returned to its former purpose, that of an adult-offenders' prison. Threats of closure have come and gone. And in recent years the establishment has been used to house Class 'A' inmates, vulnerable prisoners, such as sex offenders and paedophiles who would be at risk in an ordinary prison environment. With the crime figures rising, it appears that Usk will continue to remain 'open'.

They Plied Their Deadly Trade in Gwent:

The Hangmen at Usk Prison

During the reign of Queen Victoria public hangings ceased. This was due to a change in the Law known as the Public Executions Act of 1868. Although the debacle that had often accompanied hangings had been greatly restricted, for by that time most public executions were being 'conducted with more ceremony so as to produce a grim and solemn reminder of the punishment for the most serious crimes.' From 1868 onward all judicial hangings were carried out within the confines of the prison. Prior to the execution the prisoner would be weighed daily and on the day before the hanging was to take place the hangman would see the prisoner for the first time to enable him to calculate the correct drop from the weight and physical appearance of the person. The length of the drop[23] was carefully set and the gallows tested, in some cases this could only be done when the prisoner was out of his cell.[24] A bag of sand was used, of approximately the same weight as the prisoner. It was usual to leave the bag of sand suspended by the rope overnight to remove its stretch. An hour before the execution the trap doors would be re-set and any final adjustment to the length of the drop would be made. The rope was then coiled and secured using a piece of thread to allow the noose to be suspended at chest level.

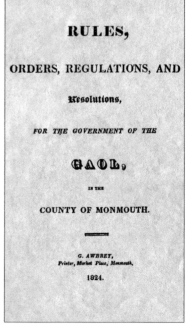

RULES,

ORDERS, REGULATIONS, AND

Resolutions,

FOR THE GOVERNMENT OF THE

GAOL,

IN THE

COUNTY OF MONMOUTH.

G. AWBREY,
Printer, Market Place, Monmouth,

1824.

1824: Prison Rules regarding the treatment of condemned prisoners at Monmouth Gaol.

County of Monmouth. } At a General Quarter Sessions of the Peace, of our Sovereign Lord the King, holden at the Town Hall in Usk, in and for the said County, on Monday, in the week next after the Feast of Saint Michael the Archangel, in the fifth year of the reign of our Sovereign Lord George the Fourth, King of the united Kingdom of Great Britain and Ireland, before William Taddy Esquire, Serjeant at Law; Chairman; Granville Charles Henry Somerset, commonly called Lord Granville Charles Henry Somerset, Richard Lewis Esquire, and others their fellows, His Majesty's Justices of the Peace, for the said County.

The foregoing Rules, Orders, Regulations and Resolutions, having been this day submitted and examined, It is ordered that the same be approved and confirmed, and that Copies be forthwith transmitted to one of His Majesty's principal Secretaries of State, and also to every acting Magistrate within the County.

W. Taddy,
Chairman.

Jones,
Clerk of the Peace.

XXV.

That on the awful ceremony of an execution, all felons and criminals of every description, be brought to such places as will enable them to witness it, and that every possible solemnity be observed on the occasion.

XXVI.

That in the case of every person suffering for any other crime than that of murder, after the body shall have hung its usual time, it shall be placed in a coffin to be prepared for its reception, and shall be carried with decent ceremony round the prison to the chapel, where a proper service shall be read by the chaplain, at which service, all criminal prisoners shall attend; and after the service so read, the body shall be delivered if demanded, to the friends of the deceased, unless ordered otherwise by the judge before whom such prisoner was convicted, and in case of no such application or order, it shall be buried in the ground appropriated for the purpose.

Resolved,

That all the prisoners are to understand, that a quiet resignation to the foregoing rules and orders, and a respectful submission to the officers of the prison, will be their principal claim to protection from the magistrates, and that refractory conduct must and will be opposed by adequate punishment, until subdued.

The Schedule referred to, by the foregoing Rules and Orders

TABLES OF CHARGES.

Any debtor desiring to have a room in the keeper's house, with the use of the bedding and furniture, shall pay for the same per week, *five shillings.*

Finis.

A few minutes before eight o'clock,[25] the appointed hour, the execution team on the signal from the Governor, would enter into the condemned cell. The formal procedure that followed adhered to a standard set of rules that had been laid down by the Home Office. The execution party consisted of the prison Governor, the County Sheriff or his deputy, the Chaplain, the hangman and his assistant. Also present would be several warders to assist as required. It was the responsibility of the executioner to pinion the prisoner's arms and for a brief moment the condemned man, should he wish, would be allowed to pray with the Chaplain.

The doors leading to the scaffold were then opened revealing the platform with its trapdoor onto which the group would proceed led by the assistant executioner and the warders. Once on the scaffold the executioner would quickly place the white hood over the prisoner's head and the plain noose firmly secured around the neck. The noose

An engraving of a prisoner being escorted to the scaffold surrounded by the judiciary representatives, clergy and the state executioner.

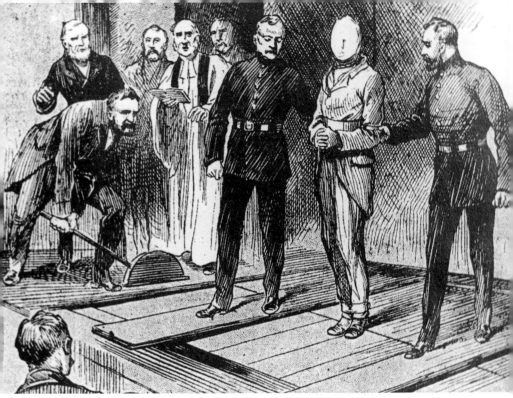

A Victorian engraving showing a condemned man on the scaffold. 'Many prisoners had to be supported during the final moments on the scaffold'.

was adjusted so that the eyelet was tight under the angle of the left jaw, held in place by a rubberised washer slid down the rope. The assistant at the same time would restrain the feet at the ankles, with two warders, standing on boards positioned across the trapdoors, to steady the prisoner on the drop, the executioner would withdraw the securing bolt to release the trapdoor. The operating lever was thrown and the hapless prisoner dropped to his death. The whole procedure usually took less than 15 seconds.

At Usk it was once the custom to raise a black flag, bearing the word 'Justice' shortly after the hanging had taken place. It was hoisted above the prison's walls to inform the waiting public that the execution had taken place. After the prisoner had dropped through the trap the body would be left hanging for an hour. It was not unusual for the condemned man still to be alive at this time but unconscious, with his neck broken. The prison doctor would then listen for and would expect to hear a weak heartbeat that would last only for a few minutes or so. When he was finally satisfied that the prisoner was in fact dead, the execution cell was locked for an hour before the executioners returned to remove the body for the autopsy[26] and inquest that was required by law following a hanging. The inquest taking place immediately after the autopsy,[27] the body of the prisoner having been placed in a plain wooden coffin would be buried within the precincts of the prison in an unmarked grave. Many of the hangmen who came to Monmouthshire to carry out the executions were once household names, perhaps Pierrepoint being the most famous. The Pierrepoints[28] collectively, were responsible for more than 857 hangings in their joint careers, although a Pierrepoint (Henry) executed only two of Monmouthshire's murderers.[29]

One of the most celebrated of all public executioners to have plied his trade in Monmouthshire, was William Marwood who served in his chosen line of work for a period for nine years. Before he became a hangman Marwood was a cobbler by trade. Over many years he had taken a great interest in the 'art of hanging', so much so that he felt it could be greatly improved. Although he had never hanged anyone, or for that matter assisted an execution, he nevertheless persuaded the authorities at Lincoln prison to let him carry out his first execution on 1st April 1872. Marwood, who was aged 54, favourably impressed the governor of the prison with his professionalism in carrying out the hanging. Marwood later said that it 'went off without a hitch.'

The only execution he carried out in Gwent was at Usk prison in 1878, when he sent Joseph Garcia 'into eternity'. Garcia was the man responsible for the Llangibby multiple murders, when he bludgeoned and stabbed to death five members of the Watkins family. 'It was one hanging,' Marwood told an assembled crowd at Newport, 'that I really enjoyed.'

During his term as the official Public Executioner, he is also credited with the invention of the 'long drop'[30] method of hanging, although in all probability this humane method of 'despatch' was probably invented by a group of Irish surgeons. This being so, Marwood was certainly the man who was responsible for its introduction into the English penal system. Thankfully the long drop removed that gruesome spectacle of a struggling and convulsing prisoner as he slowly choked to death. By

An engraving of John Marwood, the hangman responsible for the introduction of the long drop method of (humane) execution.

removing this distressing prospect from the proceedings it was, undoubtedly, much less cruel for the prisoner and far less stressful for the governor and staff of the prison who, 'since the abolition of public hangings, had to witness the spectacle at close quarters.'

Marwood had realised that with the noose correctly positioned and a drop of six to ten feet, depending on the weight and build of the prisoner, death would be 'nearly instantaneous', owing to the neck being broken. In fact this form of hanging would inevitably lead to the condition known as *comatose asphyxia.*[31] When the noose was adjusted properly and the prisoner had fallen through the trap, there should be no visible movement of the rope save the initial snap as the condemned man came to an abrupt stop.

His first appointment came as the official hangman for London and Middlesex, from whom he received an annual retainer of £20 plus £10 for each execution. Like most who served in his post before him, he was allowed to keep the condemned person's clothes and also received travelling expenses. Marwood was quite proud of his trade and believed in advertising the fact. In his time he was something of a celebrity, having business cards printed – 'William Marwood, Public Executioner, Horncastle, Lincolnshire' and over the door of his shop the inscription 'Marwood Crown Office'. His popularity was such that there was a famous rhyme about him, which went 'If Pa killed Ma, Who'd kill Pa? – Marwood'. During his nine years of public service he hanged 176 people before dying of 'inflammation of the lungs' in 1883.

Another well-known hangman who carried out a Monmouthshire execution was James Billington, a Falmouth barber. He was responsible for hanging Thomas Edwards[32] at Usk on 27th December, 1892. Although only of medium height and slightly built, Billington was nevertheless very strong, having had several jobs in the cotton mills as well as trying his hand as a collier – and according to one source, as a wrestler as well. His hobbies were keeping racing dogs, and long-distance walking, for which he always wore clogs. Married with children prior to his becoming a state executioner, he had set up a hairdressing business in Market Street, Farnworth. Billington was obviously a man of many talents who had been noted for his singing in the public houses around Oldham and Middleton. Later however he had become an abstainer and had signed a pledge which he kept for many years, wearing the blue ribbon of the teetotaller.

From an early age he had been keenly interested in the 'mechanics' of executions and experimented with a 'dummy' on a home-made scaffold in his backyard. Billington applied for the job as state executioner following the death of William Marwood, the hangman responsible for introducing the long drop method of hanging. However there were 1400 applications for the job, and James was unsuccessful.

Undeterred, he pursued his application with the local prison authorities and eventually through his persistence he was asked to outline his 'methods of work' at York. Following this meeting he was appointed to carry out locum executions at York prison from 1884 until 1892, even though James Berry, a Yorkshire man who had successfully beaten Billington to the job as 'official hangman', was still the favoured executioner by both the London and Middlesex prison authorities. Following Berry's retirement James Billington became the 'Number One' hangman and chose as his assistant a young man named Henry Pierrepoint. By this time James had become the licensee of a public house in Bolton named the Derby Arms. One of the pub's regulars, Patrick McKenna who was well known to James, was convicted of the murder of his wife and children. It fell to poor James to carry out the execution of his friend on the 3rd December, 1901, at Strangeways Gaol in Manchester. While walking from the prison to Trinity Railway Station a policeman stopped to talk to him and noticed that James, 'didn't look well' – obviously, he thought, upset at the day's events. On returning home he retired to his bed, suffering from a severe attack of bronchitis. The severity of his illness prevented him from carrying out two further executions scheduled to take place on December 8th. Five days later at 2.15am on the morning of December 13th, 1901, James, after receiving the last rites from the Rector of his parish church, died leaving a wife and six children. He was 54 years of age. During his career, which had spanned 13 years, he was responsible for the execution of 107 condemned prisoners.

The man who succeeded him was Henry Pierrepoint. Like his predecessors Henry Pierrepoint had shown a keen interest in executions from an early age. He later wrote in his memoirs, 'Ever since the age of twelve I had wanted to become a hangman.' His 'technique' was self-taught. Learning how to pinion a prisoner by using a life-size stuffed dummy and performing mock executions with sacks filled with sand as his makeshift victims. Practice, they say, makes perfect and in Henry's case this was to prove just so: he was known as the fastest hangman in the business. Just how quick Henry was in dispatching a condemned prisoner was reported in a newspaper report following a contentious trial and verdict. 'At his execution at Durham Prison on Wednesday,

December 8th, 1909, the first stroke of eight had sounded from the clock over the assize court as Atherton and his escort approached the scaffold. While Pierrepoint was adjusting the noose, Atherton in a husky voice cried out, 'Yer hanging an innocent man!' Pierrepoint whipped the white cap from his pocket, drew it over the condemned man's head, stepped aside and pulled the lever. And Atherton shot from view before, incredible as it may seem, the clock had ceased striking!'

His initiation into 'his trade' was on Tuesday, November 19th, 1901, when Henry, then a young furniture-salesman from Yorkshire, acted as an assistant to James Billington. Little did he realize that he was about to establish a family tradition. 'For the first 56 years of the present century the name of Pierrepoint has appeared on the short Home Office list of qualified executioners for Great Britain and Ireland, and for most of that time a Pierrepoint has been nominated as the Official Executioner, or 'Number One.' Henry Pierrepoint was on the 'Official List' for ten years during which time he was responsible for sending 105 prisoners, at 38 different prisons throughout the country, to their lawful deaths. His career was to overlap for almost a decade another notable hangman, John Ellis, a barber from Rochdale. For several months in 1905 they were the only two executioners on the official list, Ellis acting as an assistant to Pierrepoint. The two executioners had totally different personalities. Pierrepoint was happy-go-lucky and a good mixer while Ellis was a bit of a worrier, being both retiring and introspective – a condition that was to have, in later years, a dramatic effect on John Ellis's frame of mind. And it was he who was to become Britain's number one executioner after Henry Pierrepoint retired. It was a well known fact that the two men had very little respect for each other: their mutual dislike, it was rumoured, was caused by professional jealousy. Whatever the reason, after his early retirement, Pierrepoint was heard to say, 'I'll kill Ellis if I ever meet him again, even if this is in a church.' The reason for their mutual hatred never became public knowledge. However, it did not affect their professionalism when the couple hanged John Edmunds, the man condemned for the murder of Mrs Cecilia Harris of Abersychan. Edmunds was executed at Usk Prison in 1909. When he decided to hang up his 'ropes', Pierrepoint was only 36. He was later employed by the Huddersfield Gasworks

Company. It has been claimed that his resignation was the result of his annoyance when Ellis was given the assignment of executing the notorious Dr Crippen, a job which it was said Pierrepoint should have been given as he was the senior hangman.

Following Henry Pierrepoint's resignation in 1910, the mild-mannered hangman John Ellis continued in his profession for a further thirteen years. After his own retirement in 1924 Ellis committed suicide – owing to his failing hairdressing business, it was thought. However it was possibly through the stresses incurred by his job as hangman. He had a particular dislike of hanging women, this following a particularly distressing execution, that of Edith Jessie Thompson in 1923. For Ellis this had been the worst job of his career. He hanged Edith Thompson on the 9th January, 1923, at Holloway Prison, and she was hanged as an accomplice in the murder of her husband Percy who was stabbed to death by Frederick Bywaters. Edith was so distraught that she had to be carried to the gallows and held upright while on the trap. After the execution, when the body was taken for an autopsy it was revealed that her underwear was covered in a heavy discharge of blood. Following this hanging it became compulsory for all women who were sent to the gallows to wear canvas underpants.

Ellis visited Usk Prison on two occasions where he assisted in the executions of John Edmunds (1910) who had been convicted of the Abersychan Outrage murder, and William Sullivan who was found guilty of the murder of Margaret Thomas at Llanover in 1922. Sullivan was the last person to be hanged in Gwent; all further executions were to be carried out at Cardiff Prison. But without doubt the crowning achievement of his 23-year service was the execution of Dr Hawley Harvey Crippen who was hanged at Pentonville Prison on the 23rd November for the murder of his wife Cora Crippen. Crippen gained great notoriety as having committed the 'Crime of the Century' being the first person to be caught by the use of the new wireless telegraph system. He and his lover Ethel Le Neve were arrested aboard the S. S. Montrose on which they had sailed to Quebec in Canada.

Because of poor health, Ellis resigned in March 1924 having executed 203 people. His memoirs the 'Diary of a Hangman' was written shortly before his suicide.

The cover of a Penny Dreadful. Such publications were eagerly sought after as they often contained all the grisly details of both the murder and the execution.

The Penny Dreadful

During the eighteenth and nineteenth centuries there arose from the public an insatiable appetite for the gruesome details of murders that were being committed throughout the country. This appetite also extended to the macabre fascination of the 'Dying Confessions' which were allegedly uttered by the condemned prisoner prior to his demise. To meet this voracious craving for the bloody details of the latest murder or an account of the most recent public execution, a publication was produced that was commonly known as the 'Penny Dreadful'.

These literary gems costing a penny or halfpenny were sold on the street corners or in public houses in almost every city and town. They were, according to one observer, 'written expressly for the amusement of the lower orders'. Sold by street vendors, whose intent was both to startle and intrigue the general populace, they shouted out the ghastly headlines. The titles such as 'Headless Female Body Found', 'Appalling Tragedy' and, 'A Crime of Fearful Character' sometimes bore little resemblance to the actual crime.

The vocabulary used by the writers of the 'dreadful' was often so 'rich in sanguinary adjectives and visceral details' that twentieth-century journalism appears positively anaemic by comparison.

In Monmouthshire, however, the populace greatly favoured the ballad style of presentation rather than the more customary gory type of pamphlet. These usually took the form of a set of verses, which told the sordid tale of the murder and were mostly written to be sung by the vendor to a popular tune of the day. Given a good tune, and if sung in the right neighbourhood, the singer could sell them steadily. Nearly always the verses had a stylized beginning of which this is a typical example.

> You feeling Christians give attention,
> Young and old of each degree.
> A tale of sorrow I will mention,
> Join and sympathize with me.

After this invocation, the ballad would present the facts of the crime. In most cases, what followed were verses of the crudest form, with no attention to either rhyme or metre. The offerings would invariably finish with a heartrending expression of penance and resignation, acknowledging the justice of the fate the criminal was about to receive and warning others to avoid the path of evil. Such a rendering would roughly follow along these lines.

> Oh, pray, young man, by me take warning
> Remember me and what I done,
> Ponder yes, oh! and consider,
> Let passion you not overcome.
> I did the deed in the height of passion
> I had no animosity
> Little thought my tender parents,
> I should die upon a gallows tree.

There are several ballads pertaining to Gwent, and the following selections are a fair example of the popular verses.

ELIZABETH GWYN

In June 1743 Elizabeth Gwyn, was found brutally stabbed to death on the stairs of her home. She was eighty-two years of age. The murder occurred a few days after she had altered her last will and testament and many believed that the murder and the changing of the will were somehow related, the crime perhaps having been perpetrated by a beneficiary who had lost their inheritance. Her murderer or murderers were never brought to justice. The gravestone, which marks Elizabeth's final, resting place at Llangwm, bears the following epitaph.

> Here lies the body that lost its life
> By bloody Villain full of strife
> Who coveted boath gold and land
> As anybody may understand
> Wo be to those infernall foes
> Who dipt their hands in blood
> The king of Kings who knows all things
> One day on them will vengeance bring.

THE PONTYPOOL POISONERS

Rachel Edwards aged 26 and her servant Mary Sandbrook aged 22 committed to the Monmouthshire Assizes on July 4th 1822 charged with the wilful murder of Rachel's husband William Edwards. Mary approached a chemist and tried to buy an ounce of arsenic but she was refused and a day later she managed to buy some from another chemist in the town

The Sorrowful Lamentation of Rachel Edwards and her Servant Maid.

Penned by Sarah Busnal; The Blind Woman.

Good people all I pray attend,
To these few lines which I have penn'd,
Two criminals confin'd we lie,
Our crime is of the deepest die.

Rachel Edwards is my name you hear,
From Pontypool in Monmouthshire,
I own I poison'd my bosom friend,
And now my joys are at an end.

My servant maid as you shall hear,
She helped to poison her master dear,
The first druggist did her deny,
She was resolv'd the next to try.

An ounce of arsenick as you shall hear,
They gave to him as it doth appear,
This dismal draught then he did take,
Then soon he was in a dreadful state.

Farewell to you my cruel wife,
You've robb'd me of my precious life,
Now to the Lord pray night and day,
And beg for pardon – make no delay.

CALENDAR

OF

THE PRISONERS,

IN THE COUNTY GAOL OF

MONMOUTH,

To be tried at the ASSIZES, and General Gaol Delivery, to be holden at MONMOUTH,
In and for the County of MONMOUTH,

ON SATURDAY, AUGUST 10, 1822,

BEFORE

Sir JOHN BAYLEY, Knight,

AND

Sir WILLIAM GARROW, Knight.

JAMES JENKINS, ESQ. SHERIFF.

1 MORGAN DAVIES, aged 25,—2 SAMUEL BOWEN, aged 26,—committed May 7, 1822, by William Phillips, esq. charged with having on the night of the 13th day of April last, feloniously stolen and carried away thirty-one silver spoons and one sugar castor, the property of Sarah Rees; fifteen silver spoons, the property of Mary Phillips and Susannah Phillips; and six silver spoons, the property of the said Mary Phillips.

The said Morgan Davies and Samuel Bowen are also committed, by a warrant, under the hand and seal of David Harrhy, esq. mayor of the borough of Newport, charged upon oath with having stolen and carried away seven silver teaspoons, one silver table spoon, two metal table spoons, one silver sugar tongs, one large bottle containing gin, one quart jug, containing a quantity of lace and upwards of forty pounds in money, the property of Mary Jenkins, of the town of Newport, in the county of Monmouth, innkeeper.

The said Morgan Davies and Samuel Bowen are also committed, by another warrant, under the hand and seal of the said David Harrhy, esq. charged upon oath with having taken and carried away three black silk handkerchiefs, one plaid silk handkerchief, three other silk handkerchiefs, one red shawl, two pillow cases, six aprons, one silk hatband, one five pound Chepstow bank note, two pound notes, two sovereigns, one guinea, six old half-crown pieces, some old shillings, one pair of silver buckles, and a pair of sleeve buttons, the property of Mary Jenkins, of the town of Newport, widow.

The said Morgan Davies and Samuel Bowen are also committed, by another warrant, under the hand and seal of the said David Harrhy, esq. charged upon oath with having stolen and carried away one silk handkerchief, and about sixteen pounds in money, the property of David Williams, of the parish of Saint Wollos, in the said county, shopkeeper.

3 MORGAN EDWARDS, aged 22,—4 RICHARD EDWARDS, aged 39,—committed May 13, 1822, by William Phillips, esq. the said Morgan Edwards being charged on suspicion of felony by him committed, that is to say, in stealing, taking, and carrying away, on the eighth day of May instant at the parish of Magor, in the said county, three sheep, the property of John Hodges; the said Richard Edwards being charged with having feloniously received and had the said sheep, on the tenth day of May instant, he the said Richard Edwards well knowing the said sheep to have been feloniously stolen as aforesaid.

5 CHARLES HURTON, aged 32,—6 REES DUFFIELD, aged 30,—7 THOMAS DUFFIELD, aged 21,—committed May 21, 1822, by William Phillips, esq. charged upon the oath of James Edwards and others, with having feloniously stolen, taken, and carried away, one copper furnace, the property of the said James Edwards.

8 DANIEL JAMES, aged 25,—committed June 26, 1822, by William Phillips, esq. and Thomas Leyson, clerk, charged upon the oath of Rachael Lewis and others, with having on the 24th day of June instant, unlawfully and carnally known and abused the said Rachael Lewis, she the said Rachael Lewis being a woman child under the age of ten years.

9 RACHAEL EDWARDS, aged 26,—10 MARY SANDBROOK, aged 22,—committed July 4, 1822, charged by an inquisition, taken before Edward H. Phillips, esq. one of his Majesty's coroners for the county of Monmouth, with the wilful murder of William Edwards.

1882: The Calendar of Prisoners awaiting trial in Mommouth Gaol, showing names of Rachel Edwards and Mary Sandbrook, the Pontypool poisoners.

And when the cruel deed was done,
Like one distracted we did run,
For murder is a cruel sin,
And makes us tremble every limb.

To the justice we were brought with speed,
Upon suspicion of the deed,
Our guilt appear'd to him so clear,
To Monmouth gaol were soon sent there.

And when to Monmouth brought,
To make our 'scape it was our thought,
In the wood two days we strove to hide,
'T was near Troy house they did us find.

In heavy irons now we lie,
Our crime is of the deepest die,
This makes our very heart to ache,
Neither night nor day no rest can take.
And soon the 'sizes will come on,

AN APPALLING TRAGEDY

On the l6th of July, 1878 in the small village of Llangibby, Monmouthshire, William and Elizabeth Watkins, along with their three children were brutally murdered. A Spanish seaman, Joseph Garcia was convicted and hanged for the crimes (see Chapter One).

Attention give kind people,
 And listen one and all,
While I relate these verses,
Draw near great and small,
 In Monmouthshire, remember
A crime so very great,
Has been committed lately
I am sorry now to state.

It was within Llangibby,
The truth to you I tell,
The father and the mother
Through brutal hands has fell,
And the three harmless children
Were murdered in the place,
When thinking of what happened,
Who now can be at ease.

The father and the mother,
When found were in their gore,
Those that were gay and lively,
Wilt never meet no more,
It was outside their dwelling
There lives were took away
In a most brutal manner,
As many now do say.

Upstairs, in bed the children
When found, oh! What a sight,
And burnt and charred most shocking,
And stabbed both left and right,
They little thought when going
To rest within their bed,
To meet their deaths so sudden;
And numbered with the dead.

Who ever done those murders,
And shed their blood so free,
While on this earth remaining,
How can he happy be,
Five lives that were so precious,
Were took so very soon,
Those that were seen quite lively
On Tuesday afternoon.

After he had killed them,
And take their lives away,
He thought to burn the dwelling,
And that without delay,
Oh! may it be a warning
To people, great, and small,
From wicked deeds and murders,
Pray God protect us all.

Hugh Roberts, Pererin Môn.

The demise of the 'Penny Dreadful' came with the passing of the Public Executions Bill in 1868, and the fact that as newspapers became more accessible to the general public they began to publish their own accounts of both the murders and the executions. These two factors were instrumental in bringing to an end not only the verses, but also the gallows literature. These 'Lamentable Verses' were frequently purported to have been written by the murderer but were actually the products of a small fraternity of hacks. Publishers tried to hold onto a good verse writer, but these gentlemen often sold the same script to two different printers. They could get away with this occasionally, as each printer accused the other of plagiarizing from his paper.

In his *Curiosities of Street Literature*, Hindley quotes one of the writers, 'I get one shilling for the verses written by the wretched culprit, the night previous to his execution.'

APPENDICES

THE CHRONOLOGY OF CAPITAL PUNISHMENT

18TH & 19TH CENTURY CRIMES PUNISHABLE BY DEATH

THE LONG DROP METHOD OF EXECUTION.

The Chronology of Capital Punishment

1057 The first man in England to be executed with an axe is Waltheof, the Earl of Northumberland.

1241 The first man to be hanged, drawn and quartered in England was William Marise, convicted of piracy.

1305 William Wallace, the Scottish patriot is the first to claim the dubious distinction of having his head adorn the ramparts of London Bridge.

1307 Historian Raphael Holinshed records an execution on April 1st, at Murcod Ballagh, near Merton, Ireland using an early form of guillotine.

1312 Introduction of the so-called Halifax Gibbet, a form of mechanical decapitator.

1406 The punishment of pressing to death, *peine forte et dure,* is adopted in England.

1447 The infamous 'Rack' is introduced, from Europe, into the Tower of London, It was installed by the Tower Constable, John Holland, Duke of Exeter.

1531 Boiling to death enters the English statute by order of Henry VIII as a punishment for the crime of poisoning. Abolished under Edward VI, in 1547.

1580 A mechanical guillotine nicknamed the Scottish 'Maiden' designed by the Regent and based on the Halifax Gibbet. Is used to execute James Douglas, the Fourth Earl of Morton.

1648 Abolition of burning alive the punishment for heresy in England, although in fact the last, actual execution had taken place in 1612 when Edward Wightman was burnt at the stake.

1649 The execution of King Charles I. Described as the Most famous beheading to be carried out on a 'murderer and traitor' in England.

1686 Alice Molland, convicted of witchcraft is the last person to be hanged in England. The last Scottish witch burnt at the stake is believed to have taken place as late as 1722.

1747 The last public beheading took place on April 9th – that of Simon Fraser, eleventh Baron Lovat. Lord Lovat had been condemned for his part in the Jacobite rebellion of 1745.

1752   Under an Act of Parliament the bodies of executed murderers were sent for dissection to the Surgeons' Hall, situated, conveniently, close to the Old Bailey. Skeletons of notorious criminals were often publicly displayed.

1760   The first advance in the craft of the hangman – 'the new drop', a far cry from the later more efficient 'long drop' – is used to despatch Laurence Shirley, Earl Ferrers.

1772   Pressing *'peine forte et dure'* finally abolished in England.

1783   November 7th: John Austin, a thief, is the last person to be hanged on the notorious gallows at Tyburn.
December 9th: first batch of prisoners is publicly hanged at the new gallows erected outside Newgate Gaol.

1786   Last public burning, that of a felon, at Newgate; she had been hanged previously until dead.

1803   After execution by hanging for murder, George Foster is delivered to a Professor Aldini who tries unsuccessfully to revive him by 'Galvanism'.[33]

1814   Beheading abolished as a means of capital punishment in Britain.

1827   Abolition in England of the 'Benefit of Clergy': a loophole in British law which allowed priests to be tried before an ecclesiastical secular court. Such courts were powerless to pass the death sentence.

1829   December 31st: The last man to be sentenced to death in England for forgery was Thomas Maynard executed at the Old Bailey,

1832   Capital punishment abolished in Britain for cattle, horse and sheep stealing.

1833   Capital punishment for housebreaking abolished in Britain.

1834   The last man in England to suffer hanging in chains after death was James Cook, a bookbinder of Leicester, executed for murder.

1835   Capital punishment abolished in Britain for sacrilege, and also for Post Office workers stealing mail.

1836   Capital punishment abolished in Britain for coining and forgery.

1837   Capital punishment abolished for burglary, and for stealing from dwelling houses in Britain.

1860   July 13th: John Dalliger a soldier serving in China is the man last to suffer hanging from the yardarm.

1861   August 27th: Martin Doyle becomes the last person in England to be executed for attempted murder.

1866 Last public execution to take place in Scotland: Joe Bell was hanged, at Perth.

1868 April 2nd: At Maidstone Prison Frances Kidder was the last woman to be publicly executed in England.

May 29th: The last man to be publicly hanged in England was Michael Barrett, an Irish Nationalist convicted of causing the Clerkenwell explosion.

May 29th: Capital Punishment Within Prisons Bill receives the Royal Assent.

August 13th: At Maidstone, Thomas Wells is the first person to be executed behind prison walls, for the murder of a railway stationmaster at Dover.

1908 Children's Act abolishes the death penalty for persons under the age of sixteen years (later eighteen).

1922 Passing of the Infanticide Act: reducing the penalty for women who kill their children within a certain period after birth to one for manslaughter instead of murder.

1955 July 13th: Ruth Ellis becomes the last woman to be hanged in Britain. She was convicted of shooting her lover, David Blakely,

1964 August 13th: The last executions in Britain, those of Peter Anthony Allen at Walton Prison, Liverpool, and Gwynne Owen Evans at Manchester's Strangeways Prison.

1965 Parliament suspends the death penalty for a trial period of five years.

1969 Parliament reaffirms its commitment to abolition of Capital Punishment.

19th Century Crimes Punishable by Death

At the end of the 18th Century many new laws governing the application of the death penalty appeared on the statute books. These laws took into account the increasing emphasis on the value of property. By the beginning of the 19th Century the number of capital offences eligible to receive the death sentence had reached an unprecedented 225, these included such obscure offences as stealing a pocket handkerchief, shooting a rabbit, and adopting a disguise.

The principal crimes punishable by the 'deprivation of life' are listed below: they were listed by supporters of the abolition of capital punishment during the early years of the 19th century, and were printed in a book entitled *Opinions of Different Authors Upon the Punishment of Death,* published in 1809.

1. **Arson**, or wilfully and maliciously burning a House.
2. **Arson,** or wilfully and maliciously burning of Barns with Corn, etc.
3. **Attempting to kill** Privy Councillors, etc.
4. **Bankrupts** not surrendering, or concealing their effects.
5. **Being accessories** to Felonies deemed capital.
6. **Breaking down** the head of a Fish-pond, whereby Fish may be lost.
7. **Burglary,** or House Breaking in the night time.
8. **Challenging Jurors** above 20 in capital felonies; or standing mute.
9. **Concealing the death** of a Bastard Child.
10. **Cottons,** selling with forged Stamps.
11. **Cutting down trees** in an Avenue, Garden, etc.
12. **Cutting down River,** or Sea Banks.
13. **Cutting Hop Binds**.
14. **Destroying Ships**, or setting them on Fire.
15. **Destroying Silk** or Velvet in the loom, or the tools for manufacturing thereof. Destroying Woollen Goods.
16. **Destroying Racks or Tools**, or entering a house for that purpose.
17. **Deer-stealing**, second offence; or even first offence.
18. **Destroying Turnpikes** or Bridges, Gates, Weighing Engines, Locks, Sluices, Engines for draining Marshes, etc.

19. **Escape by breaking** Prison in certain cases.
20. **Forgery of Deeds**, Bonds, Bills, Notes, Public Securities, etc. Clerks of the Bank Embezzling Notes, altering Dividend Warrants; Paper Makers(unauthorised), using moulds for Notes, etc.
21. **Government Stores**, embezzling, burning or destroying in Dockyards.
22. **Highway Robbery**.
23. **House Breaking** in the day time.
24. **Maiming or Killing Cattle** maliciously .
25. **Maliciously maiming** or disfiguring any person, etc. or lying in wait for the purpose.
26. **Mutiny, Desertion**, etc. by Martial or Statute law.
27. **Murder.**
28. **Personating Bail**, or acknowledging fines, or judgements in another's name.
29. **Piracy, or robbing ships** and vessels at sea; under which is included the offences of sailors forcibly hindering their captains from fighting.
30. **Prisoners under Insolvent Acts**, guilty of perjury.
31. **Privately Stealing** or Picking Pockets, above one shilling.
32. **Pulling down** Houses, Churches, etc.
33. **Rape**, or the forcible violation of chastity.
34. **Returning from Transportation**; or being at large in the Kingdom after Sentence.
35. **Riots** by twelve or more, and not dispersing in an hour after proclamation.
36. **Robbery of the Mail**.
37. **Sacrilege.**
38. **Setting fire to coal mines**.
39. **Servants purloining** their Master's Goods, value 40 shillings.
40. **Sending Threatening Letters.**
41. **Shooting at a Revenue Officer**; or at any other person.
42. **Shop Lifting** above five shillings.
43. **Smuggling by persons armed**; or assembling armed for that purpose.
44. **Sodomy,** a crime against nature, committed either with man or beast.
45. **Soldiers or Sailors** enlisting into Foreign Service.
46. **Stealing an Heiress**.
47. **Stealing Bonds**, Bills, or Bank Notes. Stealing Bank Notes or Bills from Letters. Stealing above 40 shillings in any House.

48.   Stealing above 40 shillings on a River.

49.   Stealing Linen etc. from Bleaching Grounds, etc. or destroying Linen therein.

50.   Stealing Horses, Cattle or Sheep.

51.   Stabbing a person unarmed, or not having a weapon drawn, if he die within six months.

52.   Stealing Woollen Cloths from Tenter Grounds.

53.   Stealing from a Ship in Distress.

54.   Taking a Reward for helping another to Stolen Goods, in certain cases.

55.   Treason and petty treason, etc. Under the former of these is included the offence of counterfeiting gold and silver coin.

56.   Uttering counterfeit Money, third offence.

The Long Drop Method of Execution

The Long Drop method of execution was the outcome of the accumulated experience of many hangmen. It was the result of a gradual growth and pooled knowledge, rather than being the invention of any one man.

To carry out a humane execution required, for the hangman, the greatest attention to detail to ensure that death was instantaneous. Allowances for the weight and physique of the condemned prisoner had to be taken into consideration to guarantee the immediate despatch of each individual executed. Calculations to this effect were not nearly as simple as a member of the public would imagine. It was necessary that there should be a sufficient length of rope to ensure that the drop caused instantaneous death. Death was by dislocation, rather than by strangulation which was usually the result of the older method known as the 'Short Drop'. Up to 1874 all hangings in Britain used the 'short drop' where the prisoner only dropped a few inches and usually died by slow strangulation that could typically take up to fifteen minutes. The more fortunate died due to Vagal Reflex (pressure on the Vagal nerve) which causes death very quickly. Occasionally the prisoner later revived even after hanging for half an hour and there are several recorded cases of this where people lived for many years afterwards. As a result of these incidents a slightly longer drop, of about 12–18 inches became normal to ensure that prisoners did not survive. However this extra drop tended to cause them to suffer a more agonising death as it was not long enough to break the neck but the force of it tore the neck muscles and sometimes the skin.

It was important that the drop should not be so great that it *'as to outwardly mutilate the victim'.*[34] Before the introduction of the trapdoor on the scaffold it was common practice for the executioner, having placed the noose round the victim's neck, to haul upon the rope until the poor unfortunate prisoner was strangled. However the introduction of the 'Long-Drop' system providing a minimum fall of eight feet, to the maximum of ten feet, caused instantaneous unconsciousness and then death by severance of the spinal cord.

A simple table of weight (prisoners) to length (rope) ratio, provided the hangman with working gradation scale. On the basis that a 14 stone prisoner required a drop of 8 ft, calculations provided by the table showed that for each half-stone lighter weight it would require an additional two inches drop. The Home Office amended the Long Drop method of execution introduced by Marwood, and issued the new approved table of *'Drops'* to the executioner to ensure that there would be no more distressing *'decapitations'*. The 'working table' appears below.

The Home Office approved table of 'Drops' used in British executions.

Prisoner's body weight	Drop (prior to 1933)	Modern drop
14.0 stone (196 lbs.)	8ft 0in	5ft 5in
13.5 stone (189 lbs.)	8ft 2in	5ft 6in
13.0 stone (182 lbs.)	8ft 4in	5ft 8in
12.5 stone (175 lbs.)	8ft 6in	5ft 11in
12.0 stone (168 lbs.)	8ft 8in	6ft 1in
11.5 stone (161 lbs.)	8ft 10in	6ft 4in
11.0 stone (154 lbs.)	9ft 0in	6ft 6in
10.5 stone (147 lbs.)	9ft 2in	6ft 8in
10.0 stone (140 lbs.)	9ft 4in	7ft 1in
9.5 stone (133 lbs.)	9ft 6in	7ft 5in
9.0 stone (126 lbs.)	9ft 8in	7ft 7in
8.5 stone (119 lbs.)	9ft 10in	7ft 9in
8.0 stone (112 lbs.)	10ft 0in	8ft 0in

BIBLIOGRAPHY

ELLIS, JOHN: Diary of a Hangman.

FIELDING, STEVE: The Hangman's Record Volume 1, *Chancery Press 1994*

FIELDING, STEVE: The Hangman's Record Volume 2, *Chancery Press 1995*

GRIBBLE, LEONARD: Murder Squad, *Arthur Barker Ltd. 1974.*

HARRISON, PAUL: South Wales Murder Casebook, *Countryside Books 1995*

LEWIS, THOMAS: County Gaol, and House of Correction in Wales, *Cymm. Soc.*

Monmouthshire Merlin.

Rules, Orders, Regulations: County Gaol Monmouth, 1790

South Wales Argus.

South Wales Echo.

Western Mail.

Notes

1 The 1957 Home Office Act reduced the number of categories of murder punishable by death to five.

2 See appendices.

3 Abolition of Capital Punishment Act passed on November 9th, 1965 giving the Law a five year trial period. The Act was reaffirmed on December 16th, 1969.

4 Drumming-up Tin Murder.

5 Containers frequently used by tramps to carry drinking water.

6 An iron worker responsible for tapping the molten iron from the furnace.

7 In response to the request two officers were despatched, and duly arrived on the evening of Saturday, June 12th, to investigate the crime.

8 A hedging mallet used for driving fence posts into the ground.

9 Stone kitchen sink.

10 Jones would have been sixteen on January 1st, and therefore liable to face the death penalty

11 Tully's father was born in Newport and later emigrated to New Zealand

[12] Helen Barnes pledged to stand by Green following his conviction.

[13] He had murdered forty-one-year-old Glenys Johnson, a Cardiff prostitute.

[14] At his trial it was revealed that Green had had to identify the decapitated body of his younger brother when he was twelve years of age.

[15] A 'tariff' is set on most prisoners sentenced to life imprisonment. It means that after their sentences have been completed they may be released providing that the parole board deems that they are no longer a threat to society.

[16] The residue left from a discharged gunshot.

[17] Osmunde gave himself up to police at the end of the trial. He was jailed for 21 days.

[18] Later renamed Mount Pleasant.

[19] Sir William Cubitt.

[20] A system of solitary confinement.

[21] Both items were manufactured within Usk Prison.

[22] Not in my back yard.

[23] See appendices.

[24] In several prisons the gallows could only be accessed through the condemned cell.

[25] In London executions took place at 9am – only in the provinces did the 8am drop apply.

[26] The normal cause of death was given as comatose asphyxia consequent upon judicial hanging.

[27] See autopsy report in Appendices.

[28] There were three hangmen named Pierrepoint, all of whom were related.

[29] Sullivan for the murder of Margaret Thomas and Edmunds who killed Cecilia Harris.

[30] See Appendices.

[31] The prisoner still dies by asphyxiation but is unconscious at the time.

[32] Edwards murdered Mary Conolly of Abergavenny September 1892.

[33] To be stimulated by low voltage electricity.

[34] Decapitation was a regular result of earlier attempts of the Long Drop method.